THE LOVERS' GUIDE

A huge debt of gratitude is due to Rachel Shattock and Michael Bywater. Without their help, humour and experience this book would never have gone to bed.

In memory of J R, the adorable plumber who looked like George Clooney.

THIS IS A CARLTON BOOK

Concept and photographs (except pages 23, 31, 33tr, 33 bl, 43br, 47, 63, 66, 67tr, 73, 77, 79, 80, 84, 94, 95, 99, 108, 109 and 120) copyright © 2002 Lifetime Vision Ltd
Text copyright © 2002 Marcelle d'Argy Smith
Design copyright © 2002 Carlton Books Limited

This edition published by
Carlton Books Limited 2002
20 Mortimer Street
London W1T 3JW

A CIP catalogue record for this book
is available from the British Library

ISBN 1 84222 620 7 (hardback)
ISBN 1 84222 718 1 (US paperback)

Printed and bound in Italy

Editorial Manager:
Judith More
Producer for Lovers' Guide:
Robert Page
Lifetime Vision Ltd's photographs:
Phil Pickard and Maggie Lambert
Senior Art Editor:
Barbara Zuñiga
Executive Editor:
Zia Mattocks
Design:
DW Design London
Editors:
Jane Donovan and Sarah Sears
Production Manager:
Alastair Gourlay

The author and publisher have made every effort to ensure that all information is correct and up to date at the time of publication. Neither the authors nor the publisher can accept responsibility for any accident, injury or damage that results from using the ideas, information or advice offered in this book.

The expression Lovers' Guide is the registered trademark of Lifetime Vision Ltd and displayed under license. The use of this trademark other than with the express permission of Lifetime Vision Ltd is strictly prohibited.

THE Lovers' GUIDE

WHAT WOMEN REALLY WANT

A manual for women and their men

MARCELLE D'ARGY SMITH

CONSULTANT: DR SARAH HUMPHERY

CARLTON
BOOKS

Contents

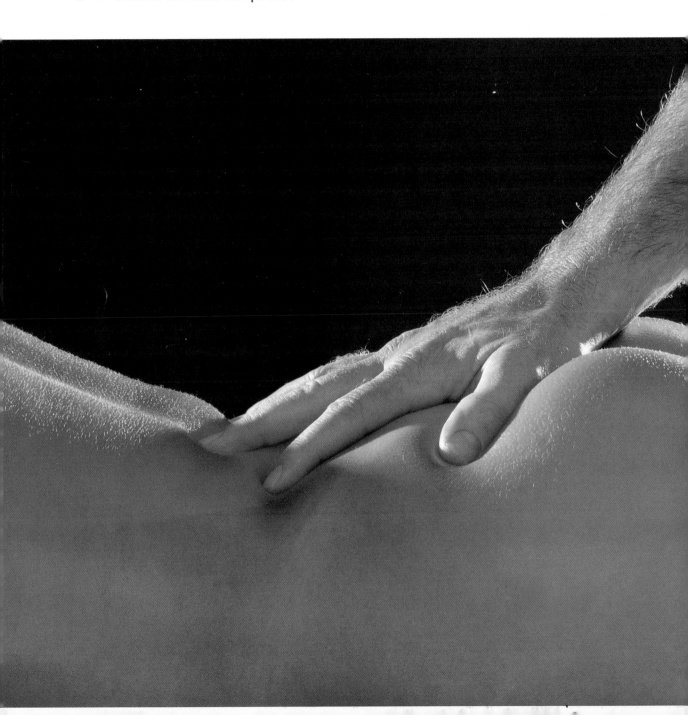

Introduction

W'ere all aware of it, every day and in so many ways: the woman of the twenty-first century is not the woman of even ten years ago. It's incredible to think how much she, and society, have changed. The question is, are these changes affecting her love life? What about her sex life? Well, how is it for you? It's not that easy, is it? Except during those blissful moments when it is.

Today's woman works harder than ever, and is even more successful. Three-quarters of women (aged between 16 and 59 years) go out to work. But we still seem to spend an average of four hours a day doing the bulk of the household chores. Some things don't change. The 'I am woman, I am tired' postcard continues to sell well.

Many women workout these days, and there's no doubt that women generally are far more body-conscious, far more health-conscious, than ever before. We remain single for longer than our mothers did; on average, women in the UK are putting off marriage until they are at least 28; in the USA the average age is 25. Now, more 30-something women have children than women in their twenties, and 20 per cent of women in the UK and 19 per cent of those in the USA won't have children at all. Despite the Bridget Jones image, however, many women are as independent as men. But unlike many men, today's woman will prefer to do without a partner rather than accept second best. As one stud friend of mine admitted, 'Even dumb women seem to have wised up to selfish male behaviour. Men can't get away any more with the "treat 'em mean" stuff of a few years ago – you have to be nicer to women.'

A woman today tends to be much more confident and assertive, with everything that's going for her, and with the world seemingly swinging in her direction. She's constantly pushing forward the boundaries and she wants new challenges all the time. Her role models now are achieving women, who are outwardly sexually confident: sportswomen, businesswomen, film and TV stars, artists, writers, models or even politicians – women as diverse as Madonna, Venus and Serena Williams, Halle Berry, the stars of *Sex & The City*, J K Rowling, Hillary Clinton …

We've lived through 'girl power' and seen a great many women in top jobs. The fact that the boss is female barely rates a mention nowadays. We're taken seriously by banks and financial institutions; we buy our own homes and cars. In fact, almost half the female executives who are married or co-habiting earn more than their partners.

Of course, an increasing number of women have decided not to buy into the traditional (male) values of success – a large pay packet and a shiny car being the rewards for selling your soul, or at least too many hours in each day, to the company. They've opted, instead, for simpler, more flexible days. They value time above material rewards.

And what about our social lives? If you walk into any busy bar or restaurant in the evening, what do you see? Women happily eating and chatting with other women. They haven't depended on men for years for fun and company.

Most women enjoy as much economic freedom as men. And they have the same sexual freedom, even if they don't use it.

On the surface we do appear to be much more sexually adventurous than our predecessors – even those in recent years. While perhaps most women don't exhibit the 'I'm up for it' bravado of the contestants on dating shows, and won't be stripping off for a man's magazine, you do get the feeling that many might like to and wouldn't feel compromised.

Bombarded as we are by graphic sexual images from films and TV, encouraged on a monthly basis by women's magazines to 'get it on', women today are very sexually aware.

Two million vibrators were sold in Britain last year, 40 per cent of them to women. 'Don't tell me,' said the 40-something garage owner when I took my car in for its last service. 'My wife's got one. Why does she need one if she's got me?' Ordinary women are taking classes in stripping and pole dancing. Via the Cake members' website, there are now sexually explicit parties for women where they watch and comment on porn videos and examine vibrators, as well as, apparently, being taught to ejaculate. Men are allowed to attend, but only if they bring a girlfriend. Yes, it's all happening – maybe not to you and me, but to people like us.

We've also seen the rise of 'ladette' culture: huge audiences of women roaring, 'Get 'em off' to male strippers; young women behaving badly and having huge amounts of loud-mouthed drunken fun while it lasts. And yes, it's much harder to find a modern woman who says, 'It's only me', or, 'I'm just a housewife'. You only have to glance at the TV soaps, which do reflect everyday life, to realize that women are as in charge as any of the men around them. Yes, they're still the carers, the ones who attend to life's details, and often the most sensible. But these days they want fun and they don't sit around waiting for it to happen. If a woman wants casual sex, she has it; she'll be more than happy to ask a man for a date, too. The old constraints of being called a tart and unwanted pregnancy belong to a quaint other era. Women are at ease and equal with men at work; they have good male friends they trust and love, and upon whom they depend.

When, in the early 1990s, psychologist Julian Hafner stared thoughtfully into the middle distance and pronounced, 'The Future is Female', everybody nodded. They knew a truth when they heard one. The future is now: women have got so much of what they said they wanted.

And yet, some things don't change. Some things in life are typical, global and eternal. Just because women's lives have changed dramatically, just because they've taken on new roles and are men's equals as leaders and breadwinners, just because they've made huge gains – at a price – doesn't mean that they've jettisoned their old hopes and dreams. Women want exactly what they've always wanted. The fundamental things apply. Women want to fall in love. They want to love and be loved. They want to care and for someone to care for them. Women want honesty, respect, unselfishness – a best friend, a soulmate. It was my stud friend who said, 'Women want romance.' He's right, we crave it. Women want sex. They want passion. Women dream about through-the-roof, swept-away sex. However, they also need intimacy and tenderness. They don't always want hugging to lead to sex. When the time is right, women want children. Well, most of them do.

In many ways women have become the people they always wanted to be, yet love affairs and even stable relationships are fraught with misunderstandings. Sex remains a tricky business. It's true that in history some of the most famous love affairs did not run smoothly. But hasn't it become even harder these days, with so little time, so many pressures?

Many men are confused and alienated by this strong new breed of woman. There's talk of a 'crisis of masculinity'. Why do some men seem so angry with women? Perhaps they don't feel as loved and needed as they used to. Don't they realize we want them as much as ever? Could it be that women behave in such a way that they seem a whole lot stronger than they're feeling? Just because you organize your work life confidently doesn't mean that you can arrange your personal life so that great sex and love, sweet love, will just happen automatically.

There are many books that graphically describe how to have great sex and multiple orgasms. They're fun to read and full of useful information, but unless you're in the mood anyway, they don't really solve anything. And isn't it odd that the men who were the best lovers you've ever had had never read a sex book?

What is it that makes this book different? This book concentrates on you, the woman. It looks very closely at exactly what you want from your lover, your partner and your sex life. We'll tell it how it is today, not how it used to be. It's not just about what you do and what you can do sexually; it's about why you do it and how you feel. And maybe what you'd like to do and why sometimes you can't do it. It's as much about what goes on in your brain as what goes on in your body.

This book is honest and factual; I hope it's also inspirational or gives you the confidence to think, 'I can do that'. I owe thanks to the many women and men who've revealed so much of the intimate side of their lives to me over the years and last week. Their comments, observations and stories are here – if not their names. Not enough of us get the sex lives and intimacy we deserve or dream about. Some of us get lucky. I do know people who've hit the sexual and emotional jackpot. Some of us make do with blissful moments. Life is short. We should *all* aim for more blissful moments.

MARCELLE D'ARGY SMITH

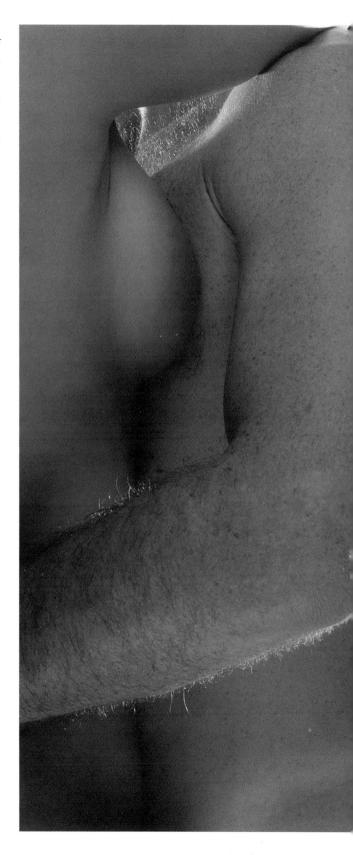

1

Know Your Body

Mind matters

HAS IT EVER occurred to you that often it's the way you feel about yourself and your body that makes you think about, or positively crave, sex? Given that there was electric chemistry between me and the man concerned, I've had the best sex when I was turned on by *me*, when *I* felt good about myself. And it seems infectious, too. Men love it when you love your own body with wild abandon. That kind of self-confidence is hugely attractive and thrilling

for both of you. But no one feels abundantly sexual the whole time, which is just as well – otherwise you'd never get a full night's sleep.

It goes without saying that you should be nice to your body. Although – like a dog – it might be loyal and faithful to you for ages, long term it's unwise to ignore it, to abuse it, to stuff it to excess with food, drink and unsuitable substances. Most of us feel a whole lot better when we follow a reasonably

healthy diet and take enough exercise – that way, you will have more energy and stamina. But hey, I do know some deliciously sensual people who love their food and drink, and they spend lunches and evenings having the kind of sex lives lots of us would kill for. You have to know what suits you and how you feel happiest.

Flirting with a man you're attracted to certainly gets the juices flowing. But have you noticed how sometimes you still feel disturbingly sexual when there isn't even a sex object? At certain times of the month – sometimes just before menstruation – you may find yourself feeling overwhelmingly horny.

When you're on holiday, particularly in a foreign place, with your body exposed to hot sunshine, and you see how your limbs, stomach, breasts and back slowly start to tan, you often begin to get excited about yourself. You aren't becoming dramatically fatter or thinner, or changing shape, in the first few days of the holiday: you are just seeing yourself differently. As you're rubbing in the Factor 15, your body feels smooth and lubricated, and it responds to your touch. Suddenly you're a sensual woman with a body that's worthy of attention. You yearn to dress it up, to undress it, to make more of a fuss of it, to pamper it, to put it on display and to have sex – which is why so many women rush to the sun to have holiday affairs. It's wonderfully healthy, life-affirming stuff. We were built for sex, and sex is an act of recreation as well as procreation.

it's about how you feel

If I've been busy running around and have lost weight, sometimes, as I pull on a pair of tighter jeans, I begin plotting sexual activity. I think, 'Ah, I look great when I'm slimmer, and I'm really in touch with my body.' There are other times when I've gained more weight than I've meant to, but, out of the blue, I've started to love my rounded breasts, stomach and fuller face, and I haven't wanted to return to being the insubstantial person with the too-slim face. Which suits me best? Heaven knows. Whatever my weight has been doing, I've enjoyed celibate months, and frantic sexual times.

It's a question of perception.

Feeling sexy is in the brain.

Although I don't deny that

soaking in a creamy bath,

getting into satin or lace 'sock

it to 'em' underwear, having

freshly washed, blow-dried hair

and gently rubbing perfume

around my neck and throat puts

me more in the mood. You feel

more confident – about

anything – if you're prepared.

Because they're so hypercritical, few women are fit to weigh up their own attractiveness. They judge themselves ruthlessly and with so little knowledge of their physical attributes that you could assume that they are living with distorted mirrors. Thank heavens for those special older, plumper women, who say, 'I look really pretty undressed'.

I know perfect size 10s who criticize themselves constantly – 'I hate my hair', 'My shoulders are too big and I don't go in at the waist', 'I've got two horrible moles near my breasts'. I have friends who hate their bottoms, their thighs and their stomachs. They say they're flabby; they announce that they've gained two stone and are *never* taking their clothes off again. Equally, I know smiley, flirty size 16s who hugely appreciate their bodies and have never, ever had any trouble finding good men, or good sex. And I know at least two men who've been horrified when their partners have suggested going on diets – 'I adore her like that … couldn't bear her thinner.'

I know women who've had
their breasts enlarged and think
that big breasts are the answer
to a great sex life. I know
women who've had their breasts
reduced, who say they always
knew that small-breasted
women had a better time.
They've become what *they*
want, and then they rush
out to find a man who likes
what they've got.

But why are women so tough on themselves about the way they look? Today there are over a million women in Britain alone who have eating disorders. Men, however, unless they're scouts for modelling agencies, or searching for a pneumatic blonde to star in a porn movie, simply don't subject women to microscopic scrutiny. Easy creatures, men are less selective and less self-protective than women. They were *designed* that way.

A man 'likes the look' of someone. Maybe he has a type – brunette, blonde, big, small. Some men are attracted to their own body type. Perhaps he's attracted to his opposite. Mostly they're attracted by the overall package: 'Something in the way she moved', 'her laugh', 'something she said', 'her wild red dress', 'that pre-Raphaelite hair', 'that shiny black skin', 'that creamy white skin', 'she smiled at me', 'I love her mind'.

Men respond to a look that implies: 'Under the right conditions, I'm up for it.' They're not picky – that's the best (and sometimes the worst) thing about them. They just want to meet someone *they like*, who *likes them* and who shows that she finds *them* attractive. It's not rocket science. Unlike so many women out there, they're not fixated by the idea of Hollywood perfection – a woman with Lara Croft breasts, mole-free, zit-free, with narrow hips and a beautiful, unlined face, who's well groomed, with no spare flesh anywhere on her body.

'I wouldn't mind if Pamela Anderson appeared in my bed in the middle of the night,' said one man. 'But I'd have a fit if she were still there in the morning.' Another man said to me, 'It's amazing: you meet a woman you really fancy. You ask her

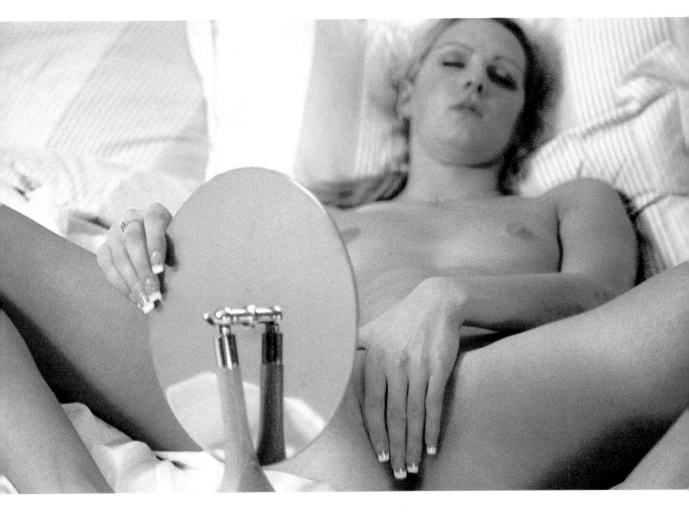

out for dinner. Before you know it, she's sitting there grabbing the spare flesh on her stomach saying, "Look at this." I mean, who cares? You'd never notice if she hadn't pointed it out. It wouldn't occur to a man to say anything about the bits of his own body he didn't like.'

Even famous women moan about their faces and bodies. Michelle Pfeiffer is on record as saying she thinks she has a face like a duck. Catherine Zeta-Jones thinks she has piggy eyes and Victoria Beckham says she feels insecure most of the time and dreads people looking at her and judging her. In a society which praises and applauds weight loss it is perhaps less than surprising that celebrity dieting takes up huge amounts of newspaper space. But while women soak up this information, men wonder what on earth all the

fuss is about. Either they like the woman they're with, or they're looking for a woman they like, and that could be any one of us.

In the modern world, when we're so proud of all our achievements, it is puzzling that so many of us still have so little confidence in our physical attractiveness. Can you imagine being with a man who is self-conscious or deeply embarrassed about his body and face? I can't. Certainly, most men I've known have been healthily fond of themselves and inordinately proud of their sexual bits. Now that we are men's equals in the sexual arena, shouldn't we take on board some of that male pride and apparent confidence? No, I didn't say it was going to be easy. Lots of us are shy in certain areas. But sometimes, as well as teaching men a thing or two, it is possible to learn from them.

Erogenous zones

My erogenous zone
Is so sadly unknown
To the average man that I see.
He will subtly grope
Stiff with sexual hope
That he'll get the same rise
Out of me.

I am not thrilled to bits
As his hands cup my tits.
It is then that he faces rejection.
Dammit. Why can't he see
That a she's like a he
But I need a mental erection?

Could a man not aspire
To aim somewhat higher
Than tits and vagina terrain?
It's the way I'm designed,
Can't he massage my mind?
Can't he start his foreplay with my brain?

If bodies they fancy
Then why can't a man see
The way to my body, pale brown,
Is cerebral stroking?
(I swear I'm not joking)
Lover, start with my head
– and work down.

SO WE KNOW it all starts in your head: your brain is the most erogenous zone in your whole body. It's also your brain that ensures you're not sexually aroused during a visit to the gynaecologist when you have to undergo an intimate internal examination. Consciously and subconsciously, it's your brain that protects you from the man you don't fancy at the party, putting the barriers up to all his overtures. But once you're aware of the presence of sexual chemistry, your brain flicks your on/off switch to 'turned on' and all sorts of exciting things can happen. An accidental brush of the hairs on your arm can send sensual shock waves right through your body; a light touch of a hand on your face can be exquisite. This is because your skin is the largest erogenous zone of your body. Touched in the right way, at the right time and by the right person, any part of you can feel aroused, from a kiss on the top of your head down to a lick on your big toe.

However, some parts of your body are more obviously erogenous than others. Your tongue, lips and mouth; your neck, shoulders and chest; the small of your back, around your navel, your inner thigh – all of these love to be touched, stroked, nuzzled and kissed. Hotter still are your breasts and nipples, your pubic mound and vulva. We'll come on to the magical clitoris in the next section . . .

Everybody has their own individual quirks and favourite places. Speaking personally, I hate tongue-in-the-mouth kisses, but I love to have my breasts massaged and tweaked. One close friend says it's just the opposite for her: the longer and deeper the kisses, the better; but hands off her breasts with anything firmer than a feather-light touch. Your turn-ons will be unique to you. And because we're all such different creatures in the sex department, it's important that you know what works for you – and what doesn't – so that you can please yourself, as well as communicate it to your partner.

zoning in

'He moved his lips about her ears and neck as though in thirsting search of an erogenous zone. A waste of time, he knew from experience. Erogenous zones were either everywhere or nowhere.'
JOSEPH HELLER, AMERICAN NOVELIST, GOOD AS GOLD (1979)

So, do you really know what you like, and where and how you like it? You think you know? In that case, you may need a refresher course to remind yourself of how exciting your body is. Your body is

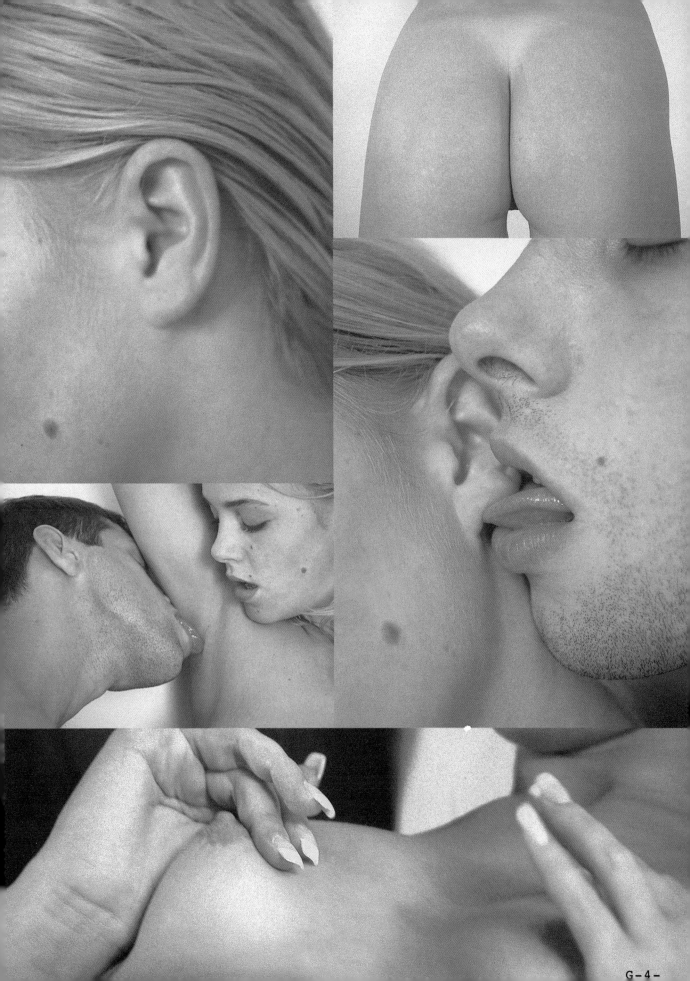

territory that you should not only know intimately but also truly appreciate. You should be very familiar with all its highways and byways. Try thinking of yourself as an explorer and get to know yourself. For example, what about your lips? Do you like them to be licked, sucked or nibbled? Do you have a favourite lip? It may sound strange, but most people do. In ancient oriental erotology, it was believed that in women the upper lip is linked to the vagina and in men the lower lip links to the penis. It's never been proven medically, but it sounds good to me. So try it now: start running your tongue over your upper lip – really slowly, then faster. First, on the outside and then on the more sensitive inside. Then do the same with your lower lip. What feels good? What feels best?

Try and set aside an hour to yourself to complete some sensual homework. The purpose of this session is to discover your SQ (your sexual quotient). You're going to explore your whole body and chart your individual sensual map.

First, take the phone off the hook. Make sure that your bedroom is inviting and warm, as if you were expecting a lover. Have a few things to hand to try on different parts of your skin to see how they feel: silk scarf, bristled brush, feather, ice cube … whatever takes your fancy. A full-length mirror in which to look at yourself would be ideal. If not, can you borrow another large mirror from a different room? Maybe a hand mirror, too. Now have a good soak in a warm, pampering bath, fragranced with oils. And then retreat to your bedroom.

You're going to discover how the whole of your naked body reacts to different touches and stimuli. Maybe you'd like to do this standing up? If you think you'd be comfortable, being in front of a mirror is useful and erotic. Or perhaps you'd prefer to lie on your bed. You might want to have your favourite body lotion or massage oil handy, but it's not essential.

Now, close your eyes. Let your imagination roam as you feel yourself gently all over, as if you were your own lover. Maybe begin with just your fingertips, caressing the side of your neck, behind your ears, your throat. Stroke slowly behind your shoulders and go gently down to your breasts. Cup them, circle them, using just fingers and then hands, and then move on to your nipples. Circle them with just a fingertip, brush the nipples lightly and then try tweaking them sharply. Think about how it feels. Which sensation is best? Maybe try some oil now, or see how a feather feels, or melting ice. In your mind's eye, colour in your body with varying shades of red, orange and green (like traffic lights) to map out how your body reacts. Which are your own hotspots? Later, you could jot down your findings and draw your body map in a special notebook.

Move on down your body. Bear in mind that this is a naked female body and it's very, very exciting. Feel its softness and curves; look at it in the mirror and admire it. Think about how a man might feel looking at your body. Stroke your belly, caress your buttocks, and glide your palms over your hips. Try touching yourself in different places with just the tips of your fingers and then with your whole hand.

Stroke, then rub your pubic mound (or *mons*). Look at it and see how it rises. Push your fingers through your pubic hair. Try stroking, scratching, rubbing. You'll visit the inside in a minute, but for now just explore all around your vulva and start to move down your hips and thighs. Feel how your inner thigh tingles with the lightest touch. Stroke the inside of your leg from knee to groin. How far down your leg does that sensation begin and how far up your body does it end? Move down towards your feet. Are the backs of your knees ticklish? Do you like your toes rubbed, oiled and massaged?

The clitoral orgasm

BY NOW YOU'RE probably feeling quite aroused and you haven't even got as far as masturbation. Now you're coming to the best part: the magical and wondrous clitoris. What appears to be a little bump the size of a pea inside the inner lips of your vulva, at the top, is actually just the tip of an iceberg (maybe I should say volcano). The clitoris is your own personal pleasure centre. Unlike the penis, it serves no practical purpose except to give you pleasure – lots of it.

> The clitoris is simply a collection of 8,000 nerve fibres. That's a higher concentration of nerve fibres than is found anywhere else in the body, including the fingertips, lips and the tongue, and it's *twice* the number in the penis.

While all that sexual excitement registers in your brain, everything down here gets aroused, too, with the focus on your clitoris. This is where those intense waves of pleasure come from and where a woman's orgasm starts and finishes. You've heard of vaginal orgasms? Yes, me too. Personally, though, I'm not convinced that vaginal (as opposed to clitoral) orgasms really do exist – like the 'G Spot' (or Graffenberg Spot). Some women say they have them and that they are deeper but less intense than clitoral ones. The debate goes on. We *do* know that the right clitoral stimulation leads to orgasm – and that simple cause-and-effect fact is good enough for me.

The tiny, ultra-sensitive tip of your clitoris is protected by a hood of soft skin. What lies beneath is an amazing organ some 10 cm (4 in) long. Like a man's penis, the clitoris becomes engorged with blood and gets bigger as it becomes more aroused. Unlike the man's penis, the blood leaves the clitoris quite quickly after the peak of arousal, orgasm, which is why women are capable of multiple orgasms if the right stimulation continues for a time. (Stimulating the clitoris directly, immediately after orgasm, is unbearable for many women.)

So what does an orgasm feel like? It's probably true to say that if you have to ask, you've never had one. Marilyn Monroe, still regarded as the sexiest woman of the past 100 years, told a friend that she'd never had one. Orgasms are, generally speaking, unmistakable, although you can sometimes have a little gentle one that you could almost blink and miss. But most follow a typical pattern: there's a build-up of arousal, with the focus on a 'hot spot' between your legs. Arousal builds until you feel you

are going to burst down there unless relief comes soon, which signals you're near your peak. The climax comes with waves of throbbing, sometimes pulsating, pleasure as your body totally lets go for a few seconds. Then the feeling gradually subsides and hopefully, you feel mellow and flooded with contentment. You may be multi-orgasmic, though, in which case the waves keep coming and coming.

Some women orgasm very easily, while others go through their whole lives and never have one (this is called anorgasmia). Like men, some women take forever to get there, while others come very quickly. Some women orgasm during intercourse, others don't. Some couples regularly come together – which is wonderful if you can achieve it – but many find this hard. One friend has never experienced an orgasm during intercourse alone, but has them easily enough through masturbation and foreplay. Another reckons that on more than one occasion she's had one in her sleep, while

having sex in a dream, but says she's never had one with a partner while awake – masturbation is the only thing that works for her when she's conscious.

It's certainly true that women, on the whole, don't orgasm as easily as men. I've found various statistics on this, from, '50 per cent of women find it hard to have an orgasm with their partner' to 'experts estimate that 10–15 per cent of women never reach orgasm during sex or masturbation.' These statistics aren't really important except to underline the fact that reaching orgasm isn't as easy as it looks – in the movies, certainly.

Orgasm, like the Scarlet Pimpernel, can be damned elusive. So how can you get one/get more/get them more easily/get them with *him*? The answer's short and simple, but it might take you a while: you have to know what you want, what works for you and how to get it. And so does he. Hence the homework above and why we'll be doing some more now. Which brings me on to masturbation . . .

Masturbation

MASTURBATION HAS had a huge image makeover since the 1960s when it was so taboo that it was just about unmentionable. Now, at least, it's viewed as normal and natural – although, as a topic, it's still more taboo than menstruation, perhaps because the major religions of the world don't encourage it. Even today, it's one of the least discussed aspects of sex, even between close friends, let alone couples. A friend might tell you what she and her partner did with a chocolate bar, but she'll never let you know about that incident involving just her and a banana. I distinctly remember a brief and torrid affair with a coat hanger in Spain, but I wouldn't have mentioned it to a soul at the time. A partner might whisper exactly what he'd like to do to you tonight, but he'll probably never describe what he did alone in the shower that morning – and probably most others. Men masturbate regularly. Michael Caine was once heard to remark that he'd been so busy on a film set that he 'hadn't had time for a wank all day'.

As masturbation is probably the simplest and most harmless sexual activity there is – it might even be the most common – it seems strange that it's not discussed. Eminent Harley Street gynaecologist Professor John Studd thinks that masturbation should have a much higher profile: 'Women should be encouraged to masturbate,' he states.

Masturbation is one of the most important things that a woman can do to increase her SQ. Why? Because it expands your capacity for pleasure and is the main route to becoming orgasmic. Statistics show that those women who don't masturbate are the most likely to be anorgasmic. Nice girls do it – and you're missing out if you don't. Not only is masturbation enjoyable and helpful, it also builds self-confidence and self-esteem. It reduces stress, relaxes you and helps you sleep. And the more you do it, the more helpful it is – because orgasms get easier with practice, with and without a partner.

If you've never masturbated, start with the kind of self-exploration and build-up described earlier in the chapter. It's simple, from there, to slip your fingers inside your vulva. If you've already had the sensual grand tour around your body, you're probably already moist inside – if not wet. Direct stimulation on dry genitals is irritating in both senses of the word, so if you're not wet, give your index finger a good lick and use your own saliva. And If you don't like that idea, try a proprietary vaginal lubricant such as K-Y jelly. Petroleum jelly (Vaseline) works, too, but it's not as good. Now explore anywhere you want with your fingers and do whatever takes your fancy: stroke, massage, rub – slowly, quickly, rhythmically. Find your vagina and push your finger into it. Locate your clitoris and rub along its shaft. Push down on the pad of your fingertip as you rub the base of the clitoris. Experts say women prefer to be stimulated at the front left-hand side of the clitoris; I definitely prefer the right. Try both … see what works for you.

Concentrate your mind and your fingerwork on the centre of your feelings and the pleasure will build – and build – and build – until you climax (or orgasm). It helps to fantasize that someone is watching and getting excited at the sight of you pleasuring yourself.

positions to try

- Lie down on your back with your knees up and apart. Or try legs down and apart; legs together; or legs crossed tightly over your hand. Move your legs around to see what feels good.
- Sit up with your back against the bed headboard or wall, with your knees up and apart. It's a good position to watch yourself in a mirror.
- Lie down on your front with your hand buried beneath you, fingers inside.
- Stand up. Try standing up in front of a full-length mirror with your legs apart and slightly bent. Lean back slightly, gaze at your face, your breasts, your pubic mound, and then slowly start to stroke your clitoris.

places to be

- In your bed – or someone else's.
- Anywhere in your home where there is a full-length mirror.
- The bath can be pleasant (warm, wet, relaxing) and the shower can be fun, too. Aim the spray at your genitals and enjoy. Power showers are best for this.
- How about sprawled on the sofa in front of the TV and a sexy video? Or on a rug and a pile of cushions and pillows in front of a roaring fire?
- It has been said that sitting on top of a washing machine during the spin cycle, or on a revving motorbike, adds an extra dimension. Sometimes even the trembling of an old bus can get you going. Not that I'm suggesting you masturbate in public, but not being at home when you do it – semi-public as it were – can feel a little naughtier, and adds a little spice.
- What about the bathroom at work or at a party, or on a plane or train? How about a private place in a garden, where you can be nearly naked and feel the hot sun against your skin?

props to use

Masturbation happens in your mind as well as in your body. Just as you need to be in the mood to have sex, you have to be in the mood to masturbate. But the more you do it, the more you'll want to do it. It makes you feel very sexual and very aware of the thrill of sex. But maybe your brain needs some stimulation, too. Most women fantasize during solo sex. So, if you don't have a favourite fantasy or two already, you might like to turn to Chapter 4 (page 92) to borrow some ideas, or for inspiration, at least. Change the script in your mind and add your own faces and places.

If you like to masturbate in front of a mirror you could start with some erotic underwear – a bra that shows off your nipples, for instance, or crotch-less panties, if you happen to have any. Then slowly start to strip off. Maybe you need some 'erotic literature'. Don't scoff at this one. Some of these books can get your imagination working overtime and make you crave a sexual experience. Or you could buy some top-shelf magazines and act out being one of the voluptuous/panting-for-it women featured on its glossy pages.

Most contemporary popular fiction contains the occasional sex scene, so when you read a passage that excites you, don't be coy and put the book back on the bookshelf – keep it by your bed.

You may find that watching something erotic, whether a sex scene in a Hollywood movie, soft porn or the *Lovers' Guide* video, will get you going. You'll gradually become expert on what turns you on.

gadgets to go

Many women like to rub against something while they masturbate, or have something pressing against their genital area. Pillows and cushions are popular for thrusting against or as pressure builders, as are soft toys, which is presumably why some very adult women are reluctant to give them up. You may find that pushing down on your hand, thrusting against a chair leg or the corner of an armchair also does the trick. Some other women, though, like to use props designed for the purpose.

Of course, many women like to insert something that feels phallic into their vaginas. These days dildos and vibrators are easy to buy, even if you're very shy. No one laughs at you – you might as well be buying a jar of coffee for all the effect it will have on the salesperson. If you stroll into any sex shop, you'll be amazed at how relaxed it is. The atmosphere is rather similar to a hen party: naughty, but not at all sleazy. If you find, however, that you *do* feel uncomfortable about doing this, there's always the Internet or mail-order catalogues (see Stockists on the Web, page 124 for suggestions). This way, you can get whatever you want delivered to your door.

If you don't want a purpose-built sex aid there are lots of other things you can try. A *Cosmopolitan* sex survey in the 1990s turned up the fact that readers were using shower heads, hairbrushes, kitchen utensils, various bottles, bananas – peeled and unpeeled – and cucumbers. Even broom handles were cited as dildo substitutes. Just remember that it is essential to wash any implements or vegetables *before* you put them into your vagina. Both body massagers and electric toothbrushes were deemed good at what vibrators do best: stimulating the outside of your genitals and the clitoris.

vibrators

You can reach orgasm very easily and quickly with a vibrator. Once you discover exactly how to use yours, you'll be able to get to orgasm in a matter of minutes, maybe seconds. Beware, though: while they're brilliant at what they do, they don't really teach you how to give yourself an orgasm because they do all the work for you. If you're aiming to improve your SQ, the trick is to use a vibrator to teach yourself how to orgasm in different ways. Then you can try your wider orgasm repertoire during solo sex with your fingers. And flushed with success, you can take that new-found knowledge into bed with your partner.

So – use your vibrator when you're standing up, sitting down, legs apart and together. Use it to the left, right, above and behind your clitoris, on the outside of your closed lips, as well as inside. If you've never had an orgasm in a certain way, use your vibrator (or vibrator substitute) to teach yourself that you can. Most men (bless 'em) assume that women use vibrators like penises for penetrative sex. You can use them for that, of course, but more often than not we use them more on the outside – on the vulva, inside the outer lips, on and around the clitoris – the places where we know that they can deliver the most intensely powerful orgasm.

Masturbation is a sexual tool in its own right. It's also the route to becoming more orgasmic with a partner. Every sex therapist agrees on this. Think masturbation, think **VFD**:

- **Variety** Learn how to bring yourself to orgasm in as many different ways as possible.
- **Frequency** The more you do it, the easier it will get. Once a month is not going to improve your sex life or your SQ.
- **Discovery** Find out how your body works. If *you* don't know what you like best, how can you possibly tell or show someone else?

2

Getting Down to It

Shedding a skin, getting past blocks

REALLY GETTING TO KNOW your own body and understanding its possibilities is a start – I'd say it's essential. Of course, many women (and I was one of them) need quite a few sexual experiences before they *truly* begin to understand, and marvel at, what their bodies can do and feel. A bit of news worth knowing and noting is that, according to research, for many women sex becomes better as they get older and more experienced.

But however much you've learned to appreciate yourself and studied yourself naked in front of the mirror and mastered the fine art of masturbation, however much you're aware of a marvellous sexual chemistry with a man, often the *thought* of getting down to it makes you nervous. Unless it's an up-against-the-wall-keep-your-clothes-on quickie, or a 30-seconds-in-a-dark-cupboard job – where, let's be honest, not a great deal is required of you – the fact is, you're going to be very exposed, mentally and physically. You're going to tear off each other's clothes and you're going to nakedly pleasure each other until you lie back in an exhausted heap, replete and satisfied. Great sex is one of the most thrilling and pleasurable sensations you experience in a lifetime. At its best, it's better than anything anybody ever told you. Indeed, you may even hold with the Groucho Marx theory: that when it's bad, it's still good. I don't happen to agree with Groucho, and neither do most of my women friends. It's a man thing.

Someone said that sex is a hurdle over which you have to somersault in order to get to know someone properly. Certainly, it is a very powerful adhesive that glues two people together. Sex is the largest single factor that determines whether a relationship may or may not lead further. It probably constitutes 40 per cent of the criteria we use to decide whether it's worth pursuing. All the other

requirements we subconsciously list – intelligence, sense of humour, kindness, and so on. – probably together constitute the other 60 per cent. In the early stages of euphoria, sexual compatibility can make up 90 per cent of the reason for being with someone, and it's a huge amount of fun while it lasts.

Yes, you know and love your close friends, but the ease of platonic friendships you have with men comes from the *lack* of sexual chemistry, the *lack* of sexual tension. You don't have to test your sexual desirability or know-how with them: you're at a safe, acceptable distance. You both know the rules and you're careful not to overstep them. And therefore you feel less potentially vulnerable. They are *not* able to thrill you to the very core of your being, they do *not* make you feel like a sweet object of desire. But neither do you feel so exposed and so at risk with them as you can with a lover.

Sexual desire *creates* tension, but sexual attraction is only partly motivated by the need for the removal of tension. We love the idea of union, of being part of another person, of togetherness, two people as one, whether it's for a short time, a longer time or even for the foreseeable future. But even if it's wonderful to feel sexual chemistry with another person, along with exhilaration and pulsating excitement, unless you're long-time lovers, there's often a real curtain-up, adrenalin nervousness when *you know, you just know*, you're going to have sex with someone.

who makes the first move?

Why should the man initiate sex? In this age of equality it doesn't have to be that way. For various reasons he may wait until *you* make the first move. I can remember doing this on at least three occasions. Once, when a man left my flat after a late-night drink,

I telephoned and asked him to come back. And no, it wasn't an easy call to make. I stared at the phone for ages wondering if I dared to ring him, but I was in such a sexual froth of excitement and there had been so many dinner dates and weekend lunches where we'd flirted but said goodbye that I couldn't bear another one. He rang the front door bell almost within seconds of my putting down the phone. 'What took you so long?' he asked. A couple of other times, when either my raging hormones or the tension between us became unbearable, I've asked a man to stay the night.

And then there was the balmy late Saturday afternoon when I made a pass at a man I knew, but not particularly well. That was the beginning of a marvellously sexual affair. In all these cases, when questioned, the men – admittedly self-assured men – said they were waiting for me to make the move. 'I wasn't in a particular hurry,' said one. 'I thought it would be more fun this way,' said the wickedest, most sexually confident man I've known.

Men are *never* 100 per cent sure of your response and like us, they don't like rejection. Also, most men *love it* if you signal your sexual enthusiasm for them. Few of them feel they're irresistible; they are scared of misreading signs. As a man friend explained, 'The average man doesn't feel that physically desirable. Even if a woman is flirting outrageously with him, he can never be sure that she's not teasing him, or testing the effect of her attraction. We're never sure if a woman finds us attractive until she's actually having sex with us.' Also, although I've met men who've said, 'I *knew* I was going to marry her/live with her the moment I saw her,' most men fall in love with someone *after* they've had sex with them.

Oscar Wilde said, 'Intimacy is the price men pay for sex. Sex is the price women pay for intimacy.' But in truth there are women as well as men who fear genuine intimacy. Both genders have hang-ups about sex, and even if we both fantasize about a sex life with a partner where all is possible and sexual pleasuring never stops, we probably mean when we're in the mood and when it suits us. Also, the idealized partner, as well as worshipping our body and adoring us, has to like what we like sexually, otherwise we'll feel uncomfortable.

why am I so tired all the time?

Ask any overworked person their sexual fantasy and you can almost hear them say, 'someone who falls asleep reading a good book'. It's impossible even to contemplate a good sex life when you're exhausted and stressed out. I know, because I've tried and failed miserably. Although they do have their place in the sexual lexicon, four-minute sex and a quick hug before passing out are not to be recommended as part of your regular routine. That overwhelming tiredness often leads to a more generalized depression and the feeling that your entire life is somehow out of focus. Sex, which should relax you and make you feel happy, simply seems like one more thing you have to do. One of my happily married friends, the owner of a busy house rental agency, used to crawl into bed with tea, orange juice and a pile of magazines during weekend afternoons. 'I don't care what anyone thinks,' she'd say. 'It's my way of unwinding and recharging my batteries. I need to be awake when we go to bed.' Sleep and relaxation are not only very important for your general health; they're pretty much essential for a healthy sex life. Tired people make lousy lovers.

should I be doing this?

For some women, sex – even in the privacy of their home with a man they like – still feels naughty. Sex and nudity are difficult, embarrassing even. One woman in her twenties confided, 'For the first few months of the relationship I'd get into bed with my boyfriend, turn off the light and then take my clothes off. I'm not confident with nudity. I feel self-conscious if openly watched when naked, even though I know this is ridiculous. I also find it difficult to be assertive in bed. Just moving away from the missionary position was an effort. When you've been told your

whole life that sex is a cardinal sin outside marriage, though, it's not easy to change.' Luckily, this woman is involved with a man who, 'was sweet about it and didn't laugh'. She says that alcohol and sex in the afternoon have helped, too.

But it's a tough call to rid yourself of years of negative conditioning. It helps to talk to other women, to read sex books and erotic literature. And it's good to realize that sex is a healthy, as well as a joyous, activity. Also, remember we wouldn't have 'family life' if no one had sex. What's even more mind-boggling is the number of parents who still won't discuss sex with their children. A British *Cosmopolitan* survey in the early 1990s revealed that barely a third of readers had received *any* sex information from their parents. Hence the received wisdom is that sex isn't a fit topic for discussion.

'my breasts are too small' and other hang-ups

Few women think they've got perfect bodies. A recent TV programme on women who have had cosmetic surgery showed a voluptuous woman describing how much she hated her body. Her husband stared, perplexed, at the camera: 'She's beautiful,' he said. 'She's gorgeous. I love her body.' Even truly lovely women with adoring partners don't like their bodies. If there's strong sexual chemistry, if a man really likes you, he's turned on by what you've got. Not all men become fixated at the sight of big breasts; not all men only like model-girl figures, blondes or younger women. I speak as someone who was told by a beautiful man with whom I was having an affair when I was 25: 'You know, you'd have a really nice body if not for your breasts. They're too big.' *He didn't mind them*, he said reassuringly. One of the things women most need in bed is a sense of humour, and an ability not to take things too seriously.

There are women who think their vaginas are 'dirty' and 'disgusting'. They're certainly not much discussed and we don't get to see them unless we inspect ourselves carefully in front of a mirror. In fact, a normal healthy vagina is the cleanest space

in the body – it's much cleaner than the mouth. Now there's a thought to ponder if you're shy about the idea of oral sex being performed on you.

But women do worry about whether they smell right. According to American gynaecologist Sharon Hillier, quoted in the excellent book, *Women – An Intimate Geography* by Nicole Angier: 'A normal vagina should have a slightly sweet, slightly pungent odour. It should have the lactic acid smell of yogurt.' Giving oral sex to a woman is incredibly exciting for a good lover. Certainly, if he's confidently expert with his tongue, it's one of the nicest things he can do for you, but sometimes it does take time and a genuine trust before you can lie back and enjoy it.

Many women are worried about how they're going to look during sex. They're worried that their face might distort, that they may scream, that their stomach will look flabby. They believe this will put off the man. So they don't plunge in, they can't let go. One very pretty friend used to be terrified of being seen without make-up; she'd get up at 5 a.m. to apply mascara and lip gloss, and to brush her long hair.

We may fear being rejected, or have a fear about being swept away. We may be afraid we like him too much, or wonder what on earth we're going to say to each other in the morning. But the most common sexual inhibition by far is oral sex.

Some women are uneasy about cunnilingus – 'I'm worried about how I taste.' An even greater number, however, dislike fellatio, and when women dream about getting close to a man, they're not always thinking of *that* close. They feel they're going to choke; they think it's unclean because a man urinates through his penis; they don't want a man to ejaculate in their mouth. Some women feel they *have* to do it to please a man, but are resentful; others aren't quite sure what to do, so they'd rather not – but they *do* know men love it. American sex writer Susan Crain Bakos surveyed 1,000 men and 75 per cent said that they didn't get enough oral sex. It's just *too* intimate for some people.

Two of my women friends are, in fact, involved with men who don't like giving or receiving oral sex. But these men are rarities. In both cases they're ageing serial seducers who don't really like, or trust, women. One of these women says, 'We find other things to do.' And yes, you can – but you'll both be missing out.

If your man loves oral sex, and you find it difficult, try kissing, licking or touching his penis first. But don't do anything that makes you feel uncomfortable; you could try thinking of his penis as a delicious fruit. Just add whipped cream or chocolate mousse and start licking and sucking. Aim to get a bit further down his penis each time. If you're worried you might choke, clasp his penis firmly around the base so you can prevent it from going too far into your mouth.

Oral sex is simply one of the best tricks for you to play if you really want to excite a man. It gives you a (deserved) sense of real power. So, it's worth learning how to do it expertly because: (a) it'll always make you feel good to be able to do something really well, and (b) the sexual rewards you reap in terms of him loving having sex with you and wishing to gratify you, too, are worth every bit of time and effort. You may get to love performing fellatio and, while one swallow doesn't make a summer, it could certainly make for a pretty good evening.

Setting the scene

SPONTANEOUS SEX can be terrific. The occupants of an office I recently visited agreed, to a woman, that they were outstandingly impressed by the couple having sex on the roof of an adjoining building one sunny afternoon: 'I liked the slow, relaxed way he leaned against the wall and smoked his cigarette after she'd gone,' said one woman; 'I liked the way she kissed him before she left,' said another. Discussions as to when they'd last been spontaneous led to confessions of sudden sex on the beach (thrilling, but you do have a sand problem), sex in the park after a long lunch, sex on a long-haul flight, sex at home in the kitchen when someone made an unexpected pass, sex in the car park after an erotic film … But in all these cases the women knew the men concerned and were, or had been, sexually involved with them. We all know about sex with strangers on trains, sex on a business trip with a man you've just met in a hotel, spontaneous holiday sex between two people who've known each other for just a few hours. Some people think it's the best sort of sex. Why? Because: 'You know you really honestly want each other and you just can't wait.'

But most of our sex lives don't operate like that – you can't rely on the erections of strangers. First-time sex with a new partner is obviously quite different from knowing you're going to have sex with someone you've been dating for some time, or someone you're living with or someone you're married to. Mostly, people have sex at home and, generally, they have it in the bedroom.

be prepared

If you're intending to give a speech, or to invite friends for dinner or to go to a glitzy party, you *prepare* in advance. The same rules apply when you think the time is right to have sex. You plan ahead so that when the time comes, you'll be ready; you'll have that sense of ease that comes from knowing that you've done, and checked, everything, so you can just enjoy. Things can still go wrong, but at least you won't kick yourself for overlooking something simple. A friend of mine once asked a man back to her flat after dinner. There were flowers in the creamy warm, modern living room, she lit candles and she'd spritzed the room with vanilla spray. She'd bathed in scented bath oil, her skin was buffed, her see-through lace bra and panties were a tone of pale mint to complement pre-Raphaelite hair and creamy skin. The couple sank down onto the sofa and then she kissed him. The man didn't resist for long.

What's really delicious is to be in the mood for sex, to be turned on, to feel the urgent pull of chemistry with a man you know and like.

They made it to the bedroom, undressing each other on the way. Because she has awful eyesight and reads in bed she always has the brightest bedroom lights. And she'd forgotten to change the light bulbs. 'It was hell. I've never been so embarrassed,' she says. 'You could have performed microsurgery under those lights. There wasn't a blemish he couldn't see, let alone what I had to look at.' Lighting really matters, so it's worth checking every room. Candles are the most romantic form of lighting. And you can have them in the bathroom as well as the bedroom, but do remember to blow them out before you get too carried away.

Cleanliness is a very important part of feeling comfortable with yourself when you intend to have sex, particularly if oral sex may be part of the plan. So, too, is wearing your favourite underwear. Or,

during dinner, telling him that you're not wearing knickers. That, according to a bolder friend of mine, is a clear and unambiguous message that you're in the mood. 'Sometimes,' she said, 'A man will look at your scarlet rosebud bra straps, glance at your cleavage, chatter on while you stroke your hair and gaze directly into his eyes. And later, he'll tell you he was wondering if you were "just flirting".'

My knickerless friend, a talented art director, has a flat resembling something out of the Moulin Rouge. There are piles of brilliantly coloured cushions and pillows on a carelessly made bed. The lights are low, clothing worn during the week is flung onto chairs or draped casually over a screen. The atmosphere seems to reek of sex and decadence. Personally, I feel much more at ease if my home is tidy; I like to keep thick, fluffy towels or towelling housecoats and creamy soap in the bathroom and I like fresh linen sheets. Just the thought of confessing this makes me feel dreadfully, antiseptically unsexy. But it's the truth. When I'm freshly washed, sweet-smelling and shiny clean, I like me better, I perform better, I am less inhibited. Many women (not all) will understand and share these sentiments. But yes, I also have to admit that I was never deterred by lovers whose bedrooms were either sparse or a riot of chaotic bloke-ness … as long as their sheets, towels and bathrooms were clean. And the lover, too, would have preferably just stepped out of the shower.

It's a good idea to keep scented massage creams, lubricating jelly (if you think you'll need it) and mineral water near the bed. Stock your refrigerator with whipped cream, vanilla ice cream, chocolate mousse and ice cubes. You never know. It's also not a bad idea to have freshly squeezed orange juice and a couple of cans of beer in stock – or champagne, if you're that kind of woman. Unless you think that bed should be a quiet and private place, you may want to consider the mood-altering effect of music. Whatever turns you on. Maybe you're going to his place? If so, it's toothbrush, knickers, hairbrush and minimal make-up for the morning, carefully packed into an innocent little bag.

We now get to the subject of condoms. Even if you do have your own method of birth control, obviously it makes absolute sense with a new man to make sure he uses them. Some women feel that this ruins the moment, but many more would rather play it safe. Just because the man seems fresh and clean, has neat fingernails and has mentioned his mother, does *not* mean that he will not have a sexually transmitted infection (STI). Do you know, for sure, whom he had sex with before you? She could have had chlamydia, bacterial vaginosis, or genital warts, or worse … While I don't want to put you off throbbingly exciting sex, it *is* important that you know exactly what you could be letting yourself in for.

A friend of mine allowed her new man to have sex with her without using a condom the second time they slept together. 'His kitchen was spotless,' she said, by way of an explanation. If he really cares about you, he'll suggest protection. And you should be prepared and have condoms in your purse, or by your bed. Remember to lubricate with K-Y jelly. And no, you don't have to have these items obviously on display. You can keep them in an attractive small box on the bedside table – OK then, in the bathroom. If the relationship is going to last, you can discuss when to stop using condoms. And then both of you should get yourselves tested by your doctor. Nowadays, it's only responsible to point out the healthy option.

Contraception and sexual health

IT'S ODD THAT a sexually active modern woman may spend ages agonizing over her clothes when she's preparing for *the* date with a man, and yet she won't slip condoms into her purse. And when the moment arrives, some women, though they may feel a flicker of anxiety for two seconds before penetration, do not insist that the man is wearing a condom. What about safe sex?

'It's OK, I'm on the pill. I can't get pregnant,' some women say. Others use a diaphragm. Some of them are *entirely* unprotected – casually risking both unwanted pregnancy and STIs. Too many contraceptive pill-takers are still in denial about STIs, which are rapidly on the increase.

One friend in her forties said, 'I'm not packing condoms in my purse – I feel like a slag.' Yet two women friends in their mid-twenties said it was just plain practical and totally right to carry condoms with them: 'I think toothbrush, spare knickers, condoms …' one of them said. Yet some teenage girls are still taking unnecessary risks out of ignorance, defiance or sheer bravado.

'I was completely shocked at what the women were up to when I arrived here,' said a 20-year-old Australian male, now living in London. 'Girls back home wouldn't dream of sleeping with a bloke unless he was wearing a condom.' And it's well documented that Britain has the highest teenage pregnancy rate in Europe.

men are self-protective ... so why aren't we?

All the men I know who are *not* in committed relationships use condoms. Not necessarily because they are protective about the women with whom they sleep, although I like to think that's partly the case. They may, or may not, care deeply about the woman. What's interesting is that they *do* care about themselves and their own sexual health. They don't fancy hearing out of the blue that they are going to become a father. Sometimes it helps to concentrate the mind to hear a man's point of view. After all, *he* is going to be the one wearing the condom, even if it's you who slides it down his penis.

Man A: 'I wear condoms because I don't want a woman I'm having sex with to announce that she's pregnant. How do I know she's on the pill? It's happened to a couple of friends of mine in casual relationships and it's awful because they had no say in the matter. I want a kid one day with a woman I love, but I want it to be a joint decision.'

Man B: 'I'm having sex with a few women. I don't know who else they're sleeping with; I don't want to catch anything; I don't want to pass on anything. With a condom it's easy: the woman thinks you're a decent guy; she relaxes, you relax. Neither of you have to worry. Bang! You can have a great night.'

Man C: 'I once dated a woman I really liked and she said when we first slept together, "It's OK, I'm on the pill." After about a month I had this white discharge and it turned out she'd given me something she'd picked up from her last boyfriend. I never saw her again – you go off sex with someone who gives you a disease. I always use condoms now.'

CONCLUSION: Responsible men wear condoms.

There's no big deal about condoms for women and men under forty, but a previous generation grew up with the idea that safe sex meant boring sex and sometimes it's tough to shift those attitudes.

They are not comfortable associating the idea of sex with disease. But the fact remains that they're easy to catch. No, you probably won't become infected with the HIV virus (although there are now 34,000 HIV-positive people in Britain). But you could get chlamydia (the most common STI); there are four million new cases reported in the USA each year. Or there is always a risk of gonorrhea, genital warts, genital herpes, NSU, bacterial vaginosis, hepatitis A, B or C. Untreated, some STIs can lead to very serious health problems, including infertility.

so take precautions ...

No one's telling you what you should and shouldn't do, and I, for one, certainly wouldn't dream of trying to put you off the pleasures of sex. STIs are caused by bacteria and viruses, and *not* by loose morals. Nevertheless, it would be irresponsible to produce such an explicit sex book without pointing out that: *There are risks to having penetrative vaginal sex, oral sex and, especially, anal sex without using a condom.*

Having anal sex without a condom could lead to the man getting an infection of the urinary tract. It's also essential to avoid faecal matter being passed into the vagina by using a new condom before having penetrative vaginal sex. Condoms or not, vaginal fluids can carry STIs to a woman's or man's rear end. The other safety rule for anal sex is: *If it hurts, stop immediately. Don't do anything that could damage the lining of the rectum. And you must stop at once, whatever you're doing, if it causes bleeding.* (See page 110)

And, obviously, you should wash all sex toys with warm water and preferably antibacterial soap every time you use them.

If you're a sexually active woman, or starting a new relationship, be responsible: have a thorough health check. And ask him or her to do the same.

Foreplay

emotional foreplay

Unless you meet someone on Friday who makes you so ache with lust that you know you're going to have sex with him before the weekend is through – foreplay starts the week before. Foreplay is being caring and loving to someone. It's the affectionate brush of a cheek, the hug on the sofa, a whispered, 'You look wonderful in that dress'. It's random acts of kindness – a man driving through the rain to collect you from work, coming shopping with you to buy shoes, saying, 'I'll help you with that report/ cook dinner'. I was once weak with affection for a man who came to collect me from a deserted station on a cold Sunday night. Maybe that's when I fell in

love with him. I certainly abandoned myself to him sexually. Men could have far more enthusiastic sex from women if only they demonstrated a bit more caring – and real liking – for us.

Sex with someone you love or could grow to love is what most of us want eventually. Some men adore their women and demonstrate it regularly. I've noticed that my men friends who are the most generous, affectionate and supportive to their women are the happiest. The women seem to glow. Every day is foreplay for those couples.

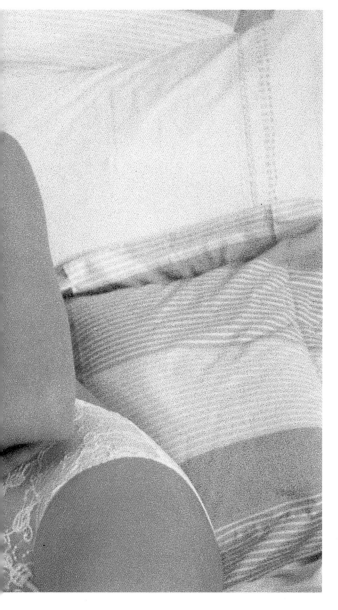

A friend was very attracted to a selfish and controlling man (a masochistic phase many women go through). One weekend at his country house he saw her reading a book and asked her to put it back on the shelf as soon as she'd finished it. 'People are always taking books and not returning them,' he said. 'We're living together,' she replied. People came and went during the day, my friend and the man had little or no intimate conversation, no physical contact and a small argument about turning up the heating. At night they got into bed, and seeing him suddenly get sexually aroused and start playing with her breasts did nothing but irritate her. 'It was like watching a five-year-old child at the controls of Concorde,' she said. 'He hadn't a clue why, whichever knob he pressed, whatever part of me he fiddled with, I wouldn't "take off". I mean – why would I want sex with someone who hadn't spoken to me all day and wouldn't even loan me a book?' It was sad because she loved him.

sexual foreplay

It's insulting, if you think about it, to assume that foreplay is something you do and only do because it leads to penetrative sex. Foreplay *is* sex. It *may* lead to orgasm. But that isn't always the objective.

It's been said that foreplay is for women. That it's something a man has to do to convince us that we're so desirable that he wants to spend time touching, caressing and kissing every part of us – rather than just treating us as a receptacle for his penis. For some men foreplay *is* an alien concept. As one of my friends said after she divorced: 'An elbow in the small of my back as I was trying to get to sleep just didn't do it for me.' Another friend reported that her husband masturbated himself for a few minutes, had penetrative sex during which time she was hugged, and then turned over and went to sleep. Yet men aren't the only ones who don't grasp the foreplay concept. Lots of women think that fondling the penis for a minute or so is enough, depriving men of the sensuous, teasing build–up, the massage, the pampering, the exploration that we love when it's done to us.

Renowned sexual researcher Shere Hite reports that many women think that touching *is* the most important part of sex, that long, passionate encounters are as important as orgasm and 'you can't love sex without loving to touch and be touched'. She also says that for many men, hugging and touching *are* seen as a prelude to penetrative sex and they only like to touch women during sex. It could be, she concludes, that men like physical intimacy and affectionate contact as much as we do 'but they're afraid to express these feelings'. Happily, some men are more perfect than others. A man who prides himself on being a really wonderful lover will love touching, stroking, hugging, kissing and other sensual pleasures as much as you do. The best men love real intimacy with a woman.

The conventional wisdom is that men adore our breasts. But some men just don't spend long enough. They want to get to the vagina as fast as possible and regard too much lingering en route as wasting time. Could it be that today, when huge cartoon-type breasts can be downloaded off the Internet or seen every day in our newspapers or on TV, men are no longer as turned on by breasts as they used to be? If so, it's a worrying development. Not least because so many women are self-conscious that their breasts are too small, too big, the wrong shape. And if the man apparently doesn't find their breasts worth lingering over, it's all too easy for a woman to assume that they just aren't worth it or good enough. A woman's breasts have a direct hot line to her clitoris, so a man who takes the trouble to brush her nipples with his palm or gently lick and suck them will have a meltingly sensual and responsive sexual partner.

kissing

The kiss is usually the beginning. It's flirting with the lips. Sometimes it's so exquisite, so involving, so intimate that it becomes an end in itself.

Kissing someone on the lips can be so powerful because all the major senses are involved. You can see your lover, smell his skin, feel him, taste him, hear him. Ninety per cent of women kiss with their eyes closed – we prefer to fantasize, to lose ourselves – while only one-third of men do so. Prostitutes normally don't kiss a client on the lips.

They think it far too intimate and romantic. And some women and men, however much they enjoy and glory in sex, find kissing tricky for the same reason.

Kissing should start lightly, teasingly, with your lips barely brushing. When you start to feel slight pressure from the tip of his tongue, open your mouth a little. He may gently explore with his tongue, or lightly suck on your lips and tongue. Some women adore French kissing – the tongue kiss (without too much tongue) that feels like penetration, where your tongues imitate the rhythm of the penis. But if you prefer kissing to be tender and playful, say so.

undressing

When you're aroused, there comes a moment when you yearn to be naked together. You crave all of each other's skin and flesh and you want no barriers. Undressing each other, while caressing and kissing every part of the other person feels very, very good.

Of course, clothing doesn't have to be completely shed. Some women feel and look gorgeous and erotic half-naked – and men like looking at us that way. Now that the latest bras enhance the breasts and display them like ripe, edible goodies it seems a shame to dispense with them too soon. Keeping on your silk teddy/lace knickers/stockings and suspenders can make you feel provocative, playful. (Listen: don't think you're sensually wanting if you're not a suspender woman. There are lots of us about.)

As he's undressing you, run your hands across his naked body, stroking, massaging and kissing his shoulders, chest, arms, stomach. Many men have sensitive nipples. Brush your palms lightly over them, wet them with saliva and gently tweak them. Clutch and caress his buttocks. Stroke his inner thighs, gently ease down his pants. Use slow, unhurried confident strokes. Try not to touch his penis for as long as you can. The erection will keep, I promise.

masturbating him

How much do you know about giving a classic hand job or going down on a man? When I talked about this with a group of women friends, some were more enamoured with their lover's penis than others. 'Frankly, I prefer his chest and his arms,' said one woman. 'His penis is great, but as it's ready for action anyway, I don't see why I have to spend ages stroking it and kissing it.' The following paragraph, if you don't already know the reason, may explain.

Some years ago, a cartoon sex book entitled *Man's Best Friend* appeared on the bookshelves, which explained men better than most psychology books. The hero, if you can call him that, was a penis called Wicked Willie. *Man's Best Friend* makes it clear that a man is two people, himself and his penis. Willie, the penis, craves attention, is often demanding but also very sensitive. The man responds brilliantly to Willie being handled with confident, tender, loving care. Be nice to Willie, the penis, and the man will do almost anything for you.

When giving a hand job, you may wish to use a little oil, lotion or creamy soap dipped in warm water for lubrication. (If you use soap, make sure there's a continuous lather and *don't* let it dry.) You may prefer to use your own saliva. Begin very gently and lovingly fondling his testicles. Take hold of his penis firmly with your palm and fingers near the tip. Move your grasp smoothly down the shaft towards the base. Use the fingertips of your other hand to stimulate the head. If men have a complaint about the way women do this, it's that we don't hold the penis firmly or confidently enough. Lick a finger and run it along the underside of the erect penis, outlining the head, the corona and the ridge surrounding the base of the head – these are the most sensitive areas. A little lubrication may start to form on the head of the penis. Kiss this softly, adding saliva if necessary, and massage in a circular motion around the head. Lightly pump the shaft up and down while caressing the head – the head needs a lighter touch than the shaft, which you should pump quite firmly. Either bring him to orgasm – or stop pumping and decide on your next move.

giving him oral sex

First, lick your lips and swirl saliva around your mouth to make sure it isn't dry. Part his legs and kiss and lick his inner thighs while pulling gently on his scrotum. If his penis is still soft, try sucking on it and letting it grow in your mouth. You can still kiss and lick it, with little flicks of the tongue. When the penis is erect, put the balls carefully in your mouth and suck them very tenderly. At the same time, stroke his penis from the head to the base, making sure there's ample lubrication. Next, take the penis in your palm and on the upstroke circle your tongue under the ridge of the head, so your tongue presses against the super-sensitive frenulum. Work your way down the shaft with your tongue, licking lightly with the tip. Keep doing this while gently massaging and pulling down his testicles. Then, make sure your mouth and lips are really wet and hold his penis firmly with either one or both hands. Stretch your lips over your teeth and repeatedly move your mouth down towards the base of the penis and up again towards the head.

For the deep suck – where you gradually take his whole penis into your mouth – the slower you go, the better. Move your tongue around the shaft as you're sucking in. Suck the penis hard a few times, open your mouth and close it and pull in the sides of your cheeks. Flick the corona with your tongue while still sucking – this may take a little practise.

For the half-suck, take the penis halfway into your mouth, as above, then slide it back out. While doing this, you could also play up and down the shaft with wet fingers. Also recommended is the 'butterfly flick', where you flick your tongue back and forth under the corona and then run it from base to head a few times before returning to the corona. You can also circle the penis with your tongue continuously while sliding it in and out of your mouth.

Don't feel you're failing if you can't take the whole penis into your mouth. The head, the coronal ridge and the seam that runs down the underside of the penis are the most sensitive parts. But don't give him a couple of cursory sucks and then few minutes of half-hearted manual attention. The assumption will be that you're fairly bored and would like to get the whole thing over with. A woman should luxuriate in oral sex, treating his penis as if it's the most delicious thing to taste, kiss and caress. What's exciting for a man, as well as an exquisitely pleasurable sensation, is to feel you being turned on by his penis.

Making love

SEXUAL INTERCOURSE *can* be the most intimate, passionate experience you'll ever have with another person: two naked bodies intermingling and melting. There are moments when you can't tell where you end and your lover begins. But at other times – let's be honest – even with the same partner, it can be pretty ordinary, a take-it or leave-it event that's rather like an uninspiring meal.

Good sex doesn't happen every time; everyone has off days. For women especially, what's happened before sex can affect what you get out of it. Hormonal changes can create unhelpful mood swings and if you're feeling tired, stressed, angry or anxious, you're probably not going to enjoy yourself in bed – even if he's not to blame for your mood.

Good sex happens when you're feeling relaxed, sexy, turned on and a little foxy. *Very good sex* happens when the sexual chemistry between you and your partner is working perfectly. The *best sex* happens when not only are you feeling good, and the pair of you have got great chemistry, but he also happens to be a very good lover.

It's fair to say that some men are simply better at it than others, and it's just as fair to say that about women, too. Most men would agree that, for a woman to be a good lover, enthusiasm is crucial. Yet most women would agree that too much enthusiasm on the man's part is rather off-putting. The hallmarks of a great male lover are confidence, experience, tenderness and passion, combined with knowing how his partner's body works and being *very* relaxed about what he wants.

Whether this is the first time you've had sex with this man, or the hundredth, you may both have worries flitting across your minds as you start to make love. Although some people are so excited and turned on in the early days of dating and mating that they don't think about it at all, sooner or later most people worry about something sexual.

the sort of things *she* worries about

Am I going to come this time? Does it matter? Does my body look ridiculous in this position? How can he possibly like the taste of my vagina? Does he like what I'm doing? Am I doing it right? How can I change what *he's* doing without putting him off? If I suggest X, will he be insulted? Does he expect me to swallow? Am I being too noisy/quiet? Am I as good as his last lover? What if I fart? What does he *really* think of my stomach and breasts when I'm on top?

the sort of things *he* worries about

Can I keep this erection going? Am I going to slip out? Does she like my penis? Does she *really* like it? Will I last long enough? Is she going to come? Am I going on too long? Does she like what I'm doing? I'd like her to try X, but will she think I'm a pervert if I ask her? Am I a good lover? Have her other men been better in bed? Is there something that she'd like me to do that I'm not doing?

major myths about good sex

1 Longer is Better

One of the greatest myths about sex is that the longer it goes on, the better it is – especially for women. This idea is so pervasive that many men have tried to train themselves to be long-distance lovers for intercourse, or they masturbate regularly with the specific aim of slowing themselves down. Sometimes, certainly, it *is* heaven to have a lover who can delay his orgasm until you're pleasured to the full and begging him to climax – preferably with you. But it is also true that women don't necessarily want a marathon sex session every time. Fine, if you happen to have a long evening or weekend ahead of you with no ties, no plans and no work. If you're both in the mood, that's an ideal scenario.

Sex has to take its place in real life, however, and sometimes, according to busy women friends with families, 'Sex can go on far too long: too much bumping and grinding – you start losing lubrication and get sore. In the morning, when you've got to be up and running, or in the evening when you are tired, a juicy affectionate five to ten minutes is lovely, but thirty minutes at the wrong time can be hell.'

2 Bigger is Better

There's no doubt about it, a huge, erect penis is an exciting thing to behold and a small, stubby one doesn't have that wow factor. Most men tend to be acutely aware of size (and yes, they will have measured their own penis, flaccid and erect). It's not depth of penetration that gives you an orgasm, though, what counts is the way he moves inside you (and you on him); it's how you fit together. Also, if your clitoris isn't getting enough stimulation, even the world's biggest penis won't make any difference. The only wow-factor penis I ever saw resulted, sadly, in the most uncomfortable sex I've ever had. It was so huge I could barely move when it was inside me and every thrust felt as if he was going to burst through the wall of my uterus. Even if I could have had a relationship with the man, I couldn't have had one with his penis.

A more or less normal-sized penis, attached to a man who makes you shudder with excitement. That's what's better. According to Kinsey, they're between 12.5 and 18 cm (5 and 7 in) long when erect, and most are closer to 12.5 than 18. Girth is much better for our pleasure than length, anyway.

3 Faster is Better

This is a male myth – perpetrated mostly by men who don't understand how sexual intercourse feels for a woman, and there are a disturbing number of them. Maybe because, when they masturbate, men often pump themselves hard and fast, because they want to relieve tension rather than create pleasure, they believe that sex with a woman needs the same. Most women actually prefer penetration to be very slow with the first few thrusts long and languorous.

We like pelvic rocking and grinding, circular movements on the clitoral area, plus a mixture of long, deep thrusts with short, shallow ones. Most couples increase their tempo as they near orgasm, but in, out, in, out at a rate of knots isn't going to have much impact on a sensual woman.

4 Positions are Very Important

Hundreds of different positions for intercourse have been documented in literature on sex. There are more than 100 positions in the ancient Indian guide to love, the *Kama Sutra*, and variations continue to be described and enthused over in the sex manuals

of today. Working out how many ways two bodies can fit together is endlessly fascinating, but whether anyone has ever managed to contort themselves into all those positions and achieve anything thrilling is debatable. It looks good on paper and it has kept the imaginations of erotic artists feverishly busy for centuries. So, if you're as supple as a 14-year-old gymnast with an equally supple partner, you might like to buy the *Kama Sutra* and try them out.

After some experimentation, which can result in cramp, a dislocated shoulder, a penis that either slithers out or is so far away from the vagina that it couldn't go in, or a suspected hernia (one couple I knew had to be carried down in the staff lift of a London hotel on a stretcher), most couples settle on a few favourite positions. Sexologists generally agree there are only six positions for intercourse: all the others are just variations of these basics.

The problem with this single-minded emphasis on positions is that making love begins to resemble a sexual Olympics; the idea seems to be that a good working knowledge of the different ways you can have intercourse equates to being very experienced about sex. Enjoying sex and being good at it is more to do with attitude – to him, to yourself and to lustful intimacy – than whether you can reach orgasm while doing a headstand dangling upside down off the bed. Yes, OK, the headstand works for some of us but it's not for everyone.

All the encouragement today to experiment with positions and to find out what you enjoy most has, however, probably gone some way towards removing any taboos about sex that still remain. Our grandmothers couldn't even talk about the subject; some of our mothers probably didn't enjoy it that much either. So many men and women of 40 years ago were woefully ignorant on the subject, and for women in those far-off days there was always the threat of unwanted pregnancy.

These days so much has been said, written, researched and filmed on the subject that it's more embarrassing *not* to be well informed about sex … so, maybe all those books on sexual positions have helped to liberate women.

Six ways to have sex

THESE ARE, then, the six basic positions for sex:

- woman on top

- sitting/kneeling

- man on top (including coital alignment technique, or CAT)

- rear entry

- side by side ('spooning')

- standing

Here are all the pros and cons, and suggestions as to how you can vary them a little. The criteria should be:

1 Are you comfortable and can you easily stay in this position?

2 Can you reach orgasm in this position? Most women don't reach orgasm through sexual intercourse alone, so it's a good idea if either you or he can stroke your genitals. Also, does the position you're in help a man control the timing of his ejaculation?

3 One thing to consider is whether you think you look erotic.

A belief that you do will make you feel wilder and give you a better class of sex, and it will thrill your man, too, as men love to see a woman getting excited.

woman on top

Once some women get on top, they're reluctant to surrender this female superiority: it's generally reckoned to be the best position for female orgasm.

How To Do It

The classic woman-on-top position is with him lying down on his back with you on your knees, sitting astride him and facing him.

The Pros

You are in charge of when penetration happens, where it is directed, the speed, depth, pacing and pressure . . . everything. As you move up and down his penis, you can be teasingly slow to start with and then gradually build up until you are fast and wild. Your lover can hold you by the hips and help pull you down and push you up but it's all up to you, really – which is good if you're feeling confident and if you know what you want.

Either of you can reach your clitoris with your hands quite easily. It's a great position for show-offs, too.

Try leaning back so that he can see everything, including his penis moving in and out of you (men just love to watch). This will also have the effect of directing the penis onto the front wall of your vagina, which many women like best – this is where the supposed G Spot is.

You can do lots with long hair in this position, too, from shaking it with wild abandon to letting it stroke his face and brush across his chest. Also, you will find that once men hand over to you, they relax, *really relax*, because not only do all their

hang-ups about timing disappear, but ensuring that you have an orgasm is no longer their responsibility. It's nice to see them lie back and enjoy it, too.

The Cons

Woman on top can be quite tiring for you; your thigh muscles in particular will start to complain after a few minutes unless they're pretty toned. Then again, they soon will be, so maybe that's a pro, too.

As many women are not sexual show-offs, it's quite possible that you will feel quite exposed and vulnerable up there. So, if you don't want him to get a full frontal of you for too long, simply lean down over him, or pull him up to you (he'll be able to hug you close and reach your nipples to kiss them). But do remember that while you might cringe at the thought of your breasts and stomach jogging up and down, he will love seeing you on top of him like this; he thinks you look incredibly sexy. There is

another neat way around this: keep some clothes on – his white shirt, perhaps, or, if you are feeling bolder, maybe a little basque.

Variations

From kneeling astride him, try tipping forward over his chest so that you can kiss him. Or, you could go down with your legs out behind you and rest on your elbows over him (the missionary position with the roles reversed). Squeeze your legs together in this position if you want to maximize pressure on your vulva and clitoral area.

The other main variation of this position is to kneel astride him, but facing his toes instead. Then you can lean back a little, stay upright or lean right forward (and every position in between). This will present him with your perineum and anal area, which he can stroke and massage. Watch out for the slip-out factor, though – very hard erections can't flex too far.

You can also try squatting over him, either way round, rather than kneeling. It's even more tiring on your muscles but maybe it'll work for you. If you like deep penetration, sit over him sideways on, so that you can raise one of his legs up to your chest and then you can push right down into his groin area.

sitting/kneeling

These are basically all variations of the previous positions (for example, woman on top facing him, or woman on top with her back to him), but because so many lovers are fond of sitting and kneeling positions they get a heading of their own.

The classic sitting position is for you to sit on him while he sits on a chair, either facing him or with your back to him. Or, you sit on the end of the bed while he kneels in front of you. Or, you kneel on a chair or on the side of the bed while he stands and enters you from behind. Or, he kneels between your thighs and pulls you up to him while you lie on your back. Or, he kneels while you straddle him face-to-face. You get the idea probably. If you crave more variety, you simply move around the place and view the stunning potential of each room.

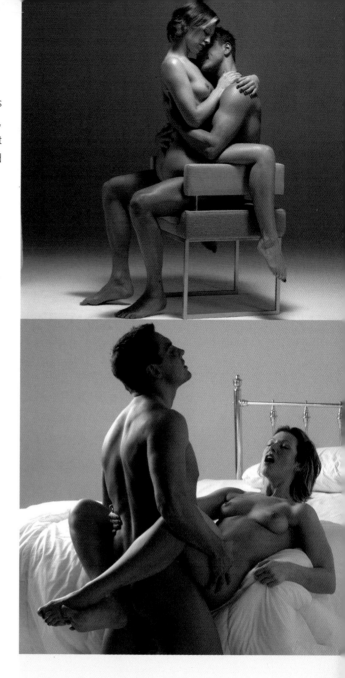

man on top

This includes everything from the undeservedly derided, classic missionary position (named, so the story goes, after the missionaries to the Pacific Islands, who used it) to the newfangled, hard-to-pull-off coital alignment technique (page 49).

How To Do It

The woman lies on her back with her legs apart and the man lowers himself down on top of her with his legs between hers.

The Pros

It's easy and obvious, so it's great for beginners, for quickies, and for when you just want simple sex. It's also the most intimate position: you can see his face, look into his eyes and kiss. Because the man controls the depth and pace of intercourse – and he can easily pull out if he's coming too quickly – it's a good position for fast ejaculators.

This is the best position if you're feeling self-conscious about your weight or the size of your stomach (but most men aren't too analytical about your body when they're having sex). And it's a relaxing position for the woman. But you'll get far more out of it if you thrust your pelvis up to meet him, grab his buttocks, push him where you want him to go and move your body in rhythm with his.

> It's the best position for the male orgasm: many men change to the missionary when they're ready to come.

The Cons

Not only can you not control the action when you're underneath – other than by changing the rhythm in which you're moving with him – nor can you move a great deal. You both have to bear his weight to some degree, which is tiring, and if he's overweight, this can be a really tough position. But

he shouldn't just be lying on top of you – he should raise himself onto his elbows or his hands, and it's a help if he does. Unless he makes a determined effort to keep a rhythmic pressure in front of your vagina (not easy), it's not a great position for clitoral stimulation. Also, it's not that easy for your hands to slip in and help out.

Variations

To increase the pressure and friction, you can close your legs together so that his legs are on the outside. You open your legs and raise your knees, keeping your feet on the bed (this gives better penetration). Try crossing your feet behind his back. This feels sexy and gives good penetration, but it does limit movement. You can raise your legs up and rest them on his shoulders before you start – you need to be flexible, but you'll get deeper penetration. Or you can raise both legs vertically in the air. If you just raise one leg over his shoulder, it will allow him to move around quite a lot and therefore find the angles and places that please you most.

It's worth experimenting with pillows under your bottom – for better alignment. Or you might like to try lying on your back on the bed and lowering your head and arms until they rest on the floor – standing on your head, as it were. The blood will rush to your head pretty quickly, so you won't want to stay down there for too long, but this does tend to produce memorable orgasms.

Man on top is more relaxing for

women than some positions, too.

But you shouldn't just lie there.

Rear entry lets men view their

own performance stroke by stroke

without you knowing what they're

up to behind your back.

The Coital Alignment Technique (CAT)

If CAT does suit you as a couple, your sex life will definitely reach a higher plane as you're more likely to have simultaneous orgasms when you use it. When Edward Eichel first wrote about his new coital alignment technique in the early 1990s, everybody was talking about it, and when a tried-and-tested, step-by-step guide was published in *Cosmopolitan*, the magazine had more requests for reprint and syndication than ever before in its history. It is, however, quite hard to master and not everyone has the patience. So, it's not what you'd want to choose for sex with a brand-new lover.

It's more about the movement and creating pressure in the right place than the position – which is why many men don't take to it. Thrusting is forbidden. But the rocking and rolling motion this technique uses is excellent for stimulating the clitoris, just where you want it, with a firm, rhythmic pressure.

How To Do It

Get yourselves into the basic missionary position. Then ask your lover to move up and forward over you a little, so that the shaft of his penis is mainly outside your vagina and resting against your pubic mound. He should let all his weight rest on you. Then you start the rocking and rolling. The woman should lead the upward stroke: you push up and forward with your pelvis so that his penis re-enters your vagina while he keeps the pressure on.

He then leads the downward stroke, rocking forward and letting his penis slide out of you again, by pushing your pelvis back and down again, while you concentrate on keeping your clitoris pressed against him the whole time.

Find a steady, even pace and keep it going until you reach orgasm: no speeding up allowed and no thrusting. It sounds complicated, and it is, but if you both focus on the goal of rhythmic pressure on the clitoris, you'll get there eventually.

rear entry

You'll either love this this position or hate it. Some women resent it because of its lack of romantic intimacy, while some deem it plain uncivilized. If, however, you get to like it, you'll be in agreement with the legions of men who cite this as their favourite position. Most men find it incredibly exciting, probably because it seems more lusty and animal-like than any other.

For something more intimate and sensual, try a lateral entry position. You lie on your back and lift your legs over his hips and thighs while he lies sideways on, facing you. This way you get some of the rear entry benefits without any of the potential anxieties.

How To Do It

There are quite a few variations on this one, but the classic 'doggie position' is with you on your hands and knees while he kneels behind you and enters you from the rear. You may also lower your upper body so that your chest touches the bed and your buttocks are thrust towards him.

The Pros

He can penetrate very deeply and women feel it more profoundly than in any other position. Orgasms also feel more intense because this position directs his penis onto the front wall of your vagina. His hands are free to hold your breasts or stimulate your clitoris, too. Men get very excited about this one because they can watch their own performance in private, because you don't know what they're up to behind your back. He'll love to feel this dominance, and you can surrender to his thrusts completely and get utterly swept away.

The Cons

If he's big and you're small, thrusting in this position can feel uncomfortable, even to the point that it is painful. One of my women friends also reported feeling hugely self-conscious, and embarrassed about her swinging breasts and sagging tummy.

Variations

Lie on your stomach, raised up on your elbows so he gets a tight entry from behind and between your legs, but takes his own upper body weight on his hands. Or try it with you lying flat and with your legs apart. Alternatively, you might like to stand up and bend over at the waist (lean on a wall or flop forward onto a bed) while he stands and enters from behind you. If you are very flexible, you can bend right over to touch the floor, with your legs apart or together (hang onto one of the bed legs or something). 'The wheelbarrow' is yet one more variation, where you lie across the bed and he lifts your legs and holds you up, so that your legs – resting on his hips – are stretched out behind him like the handles of a barrow.

side by side

This is a cosy, lazy position, but it leaves your hands free to caress, stroke and hug, and there's lots of full-body contact. Side by side is great for early mornings, or when you're tired, because it's lovemaking that feels warm and affectionate.

How To Do It

The main position is also called 'spoons' because the shape of your bodies resembles two spoons lying neatly nestled together, side-by-side in a drawer, fitting perfectly into each other's curves. To start, either roll out of a rear entry position (see above) or, to begin in this position, raise your knees so that he can enter you from behind and below. His arms wrap around you and hug you closely to him. To keep him inside you'll need to push your bottom out and towards him and keep your top knee pointing forwards.

The Pros

It's huggy, cuddly, and makes you feel safe. As your face is turned away from him, you can drift off somewhere in your imagination if you want to. His hands are free enough to reach a lot of your body, whether it's to clasp you tightly or to rub your clitoris. He can kiss your neck and cup and stroke your breasts. This position is good if you want to slow things down because the rhythm here tends to be relatively slow. It is also *very* nice to be able to fall asleep together in this position afterwards.

The Cons

Not a good one to choose for a quickie. It's not the easiest position, either, as you need to pretty careful about angling yourselves towards each other if you want to get in and stay in. Penetration is limited, too.

Variations

The best variation is to curl down and away from him so that your back is at right angles to his chest and your legs slide through his. This presses your whole pubic area more directly onto his and you can grind on him more firmly.

The pace tends to be slower in the
spoons position, so it's a good one
if you want to slow things down
and have gentle, easy sex.

Standing

Sometimes, it's the only way.

How To Do It

This can get dangerously wobbly: when you're both upright, you'll need a wall to support you. If you go for the face-to-face option, you lean back against a wall while he stands between your legs and pulls you onto him. Or lean forward onto the wall (washing machine, sink, whatever) and stick your bottom out while he enters you from behind.

The Pros

Good for urgent sex – you can do it anywhere and you don't even have to take your clothes off. It's great for lustful quickies.

The Cons

Wobbly, uncomfortable and there's a good chance of fall-out if you're both standing.

Why Bother?

It's fun. It's a huge amount of fun.

Variations

To reduce the wobble factor, keep him standing while you lie back on something (for front entry), or bend forward (for rear entry).

You could lie back on the bed
with your feet on the ground, or
try lying on a tabletop with your
heels on his shoulders. Or lie
back on the side of a bed while
he pushes your legs towards
your chest so that he can
stand and deliver.

3

Getting it On

get a fabulous reaction after a very few minutes. The only time he may refuse to be aroused is when he's watching the World Cup. When that's the case, be prepared to wait not only for full time but also allow a few extra minutes for injury time, post-match commentary and interviews.

A man who confidently knows how to handle you in bed is a real turn-on. Someone who gazes directly into your eyes, someone who lies on his side looking at you draped sideways and strokes you from your breast along your torso, down to your waist, across your bottom, across your thighs to your knees and maybe down to your toes.

A man who says, 'I love your body; I love every curve ... I love your breasts, your hips, your stomach, your shoulders, your thighs,' is a turn-on because we never tire of hearing it and it's so hard to believe and so wonderful when a man says it, and they don't say it often enough. The more erogenous the zone, the more exciting it is to hear it mentioned out loud. Unsurprisingly, biological terminology like 'vagina' is used by very few men; even 'clitoris' doesn't crop up that often. 'Clit', possibly, but even that's rare. Some women are incredibly turned on by such words as 'pussy', 'cunt', 'cock', 'prick', or 'fuck', as the man describes what he'd like to be doing to them. Others recoil slightly. While they may crave the whole menu of sexual possibilities, they prefer to experience them in silence. Or they may just prefer the commentary to be less porno flick and more in line with what they fondly imagine Hugh Grant might say.

Let's face it, who isn't going to be turned on by a man with an educated tongue that licks and flicks and explores, and who clearly adores driving you wild with cunnilingus? And it's g-o-o-d when he looks up and says you taste of honey. The sight of your naked lover lit by the glow of candlelight, standing with his penis erect and waiting, and you sinking to your knees and kissing it, taking it in your mouth and savouring it, and getting him to the point where he can't resist you – that's a turn-on.

But some men are more intuitive than others, or simply have an inborn ability to read a woman's sexual mind and they can be three jumps ahead of her. Sometimes you don't know what turns you on until it's happening to you. And some things do definitely turn you off. Whether it's bad breath, bondage or buggery, you do have to *communicate* to the man what you do and don't like.

You're both on a learning curve. But is it possible to train a man to please you? Sounds patronizing? Well, think about it.

What you do have to remember is that most men yearn to be good lovers; they're quite competitive about it – like they are about 'size'. Even though, initially, there were a few raised eyebrows and no-no nods when I asked men friends if it were possible to 'train' them in bed, after a few glasses of wine and some probing discussion, they agreed that yes, in fact, there were ways of suggesting things.

Training your man

ASK A MAN, any man who truly likes women and understands them, if his sexual partners ever said what they wanted in bed. 'No,' he'll say. 'Women hate talking about stuff like that.' 'So what do you do?' I ask. 'You ask the woman what *she* likes. You say, "Does it feel good?" You try various positions, pressures, moves, strokes, and you keep asking her how it feels.' 'But what if she wanted something done differently, or preferred something else and she didn't like to ask?' 'Look,' he says, 'I communicate, I ask all the questions I can think of, but I can't run through the entire sexual repertoire. It's nearly always me doing the talking and asking. Women may make those nice moans – you interpret the depth and tone of the moan and work out the pleasure factor they're getting. They say, "Don't stop!" or "More!", which is helpful. They get into a position where it's reasonably obvious what they'd like you to do. Or you adjust or roll them into a position you think they're going to enjoy. But hardly any of them actually open their mouths to *tell* you what they want. You just have to assume that you're giving a woman what she wants and enjoys unless she tells you otherwise. I haven't had too many complaints.'

Few women would complain of this sort of treatment. This is a man who knows how to talk to a woman, a man who takes pride in being a good lover, a man whose genuine pleasure comes from pleasuring his partner. Such men, as we know, do not grow on trees. Most men need training. Why should even the most sexually sophisticated of them be expected to guess our own particular needs? Men would say, correctly, that most women need training as well. But it's strange, isn't it, that however aware the modern woman is, she is still, mostly, reluctant to tell her partner what she wants. Why is this? In Shere Hite's latest Hite Report on Female Sexuality, Dr Pepper Schwartz points out that even when women are no longer economically dependent, they are still used to modifying their sexual desire to fit their more important needs.

When most of us these days have our own careers and jobs and can pay our way, what *are* a woman's most important needs? Probably, we need to be assured of the continuing love of a man. Some women think that they may jeopardize that love in some way if they're too 'demanding' or 'assertive', or if they are seen to 'challenge' the man sexually. In other words, it's still so ingrained in us that generally in life we're the ones who have to please men, that many of us wouldn't *dream* of saying what we wanted in bed. If sex were regarded as food, then some of us are prepared to eat what's placed in front of us – whatever it is and however it's served.

Why are we so shy and so reluctant to tell men what we want? A discussion on the subject, among a group of women aged between 23 and 56, elicited the following comments:

1 He'd get offended.
2 I don't want to imply that he's no good in bed.
3 We never talk to one another during sex until he says, 'I'm coming.'
4 You can't tell a man what to do.
5 He's interested in pleasing himself, not me, but it only lasts four minutes. (If your 'important needs' are a sports car, designer clothes and an apartment with a view of the river and he's paying, it's highly likely that training him to please you sexually won't be an issue. You'll lie back and think of Hermès.)
6 It's never occurred to me to tell him what I wanted. I'm sure he'd love it.
7 He'd get upset; he might even get supersensitive and back off completely.
8 I hate talking about sex during sex because it seems so mechanical.

9 It would break the romantic spell, wouldn't it?

10 We haven't slept together for years. It would be a dreadful shock if one of us suggested it. It would ruin a very pleasant arrangement.

11 I *love* sex with him. It's never occurred to me that it could be *better*.

12 It's always been great. He's instinctively good – he's shown me what to do, or made suggestions. I'm the one on the learning curve. But if anything happens to us, I'm definitely up for training the next man.

13 I'm not sure what I'd like him to do, so how do I know what to tell him?

14 I do wish he wouldn't answer his mobile when we're having sex.

15 We have a great sex life but I don't think I've got the courage or balls, or whatever it takes, to really go for some of my fantasies.

As the meeting continued, a couple of women in the group said that whenever they felt *very* bold and turned on, they had made 'reasonably erotic or disgusting' suggestions with excellent results. Most women thought the word 'training' sounded patronizing, as if we were talking about training dogs. Someone said that was exactly what it was like. But think how people love their dogs and how necessary it is to train them so that they know what is, and is not, acceptable behaviour. There was general consensus that we should try to find a way to talk to our partners and communicate our desires more than we do – despite general reluctance and some shyness. It was agreed that there'd been too much lazy, selfish male sexual behaviour that we'd let pass without comment – except for one woman, who'd said, after a *very* brief encounter, 'Is that it?'

It was also noted that not all men were designed to be good lovers and maybe we'd have to embrace their 'other sterling qualities'. This produced groans from three women in long-term relationships who said that perhaps they needed to have an affair. For the rest of us, there was mild incredulity that, now we came to think of it, we *didn't* ask for what we wanted. We resolved to start communicating with our partners and the motion was carried.

the man's point of view

One male friend said, 'It's dead easy: there are nine words a woman needs to train a man.' 'Nine words, eh?' He nodded, 'Up, down, left, right, harder, softer, faster, slower, deeper.' 'Yes,' I said. 'It's a start – one that I believe that some of us, even the shy ones, may have made.' 'Men don't at all mind being told what to do,' said my male friend. 'But you put it to them in such a way that they think it's their suggestion. For instance, you look a man in the eye and you purr at him, "I know what you'd *love* to do to me." Then, if you want him to take you from behind, tie you to the bedpost or go to the kitchen and fetch you a drink, you'll find he'll respond.'

Another man, who baulked at first when he heard me mention training, thought about it for a moment and then summed up how he thought the average man would react: 'Well, obviously it's possible, if you intersperse the "training" with masses of praise and encouragement. I don't mean that you want a running commentary about your progress, but if, say, you're giving her oral sex, it'd be great to hear that she loves what you're doing. If she says, "I love it when you flick your tongue", you know to flick – if you're not already. If she wants you to stop, she could say, "You drive me wild when you do … [something else]." A man would be thrilled to do that "something else". Men are sensitive about performance, so if she says, "It's so good when you lick on the left, or suck [whatever she wants]" – she's telling me I'm a great lover.'

'Look, men don't want masses of instructions, [just] one at a time. Then say how it feels. Some women want you to do wild and wonderful things to them – you can't guess. Some women like one finger in their vagina, some two and some, frankly, like a little more. Different women like different things. But a man wouldn't push his chances on something like that. She'd have to spell it out slowly and surely.'

'If you're being told you're an incredible lover – yes, I know it's the old "Nobody does it better" line, but men love hearing it – you really do pull out the stops to give her what she wants.' When I put it to him that maybe it *was* like training a dog, he replied, 'Of course it is. You say "Good boy" to a dog, and give him chocolate drops to reward him for good behaviour. Men like to be rewarded too.'

Further hints in man-training

YOU MAY – *may* – be lucky enough to find a man who is either a naturally good lover or who has been well trained in the past, but even *he* won't be able to do everything just as you like it, straight out of the box, so to speak. Why? Because women are all different. We've all, too – unless we've been very lucky – had experience of the 'Man Who Knows He is Good in Bed'. Hell, isn't it? Twiddle this, stroke that, fiddle with the other, count to five, swap sides and in … then 'How was it for you?'

What some women like, others find a complete turn-off. Men, too, vary in their likes but not nearly as much as women. It's not demeaning in any way at all to say that men are, sexually speaking, fairly simple souls. Ask any hooker what her clients really want and she'll tell you, 'It's simple: they want to feel they've turned me on and brought me off.' And when I talk about training your man as you'd train a dog, I don't mean that men are like dogs, just that all animals, including humans, respond positively to the same thing: a reward when they've done well.

touching

Men want to please … yet it's almost as though they don't know what they're allowed to do. Most of us love to be touched, stroked, fondled and generally made a fuss of … everywhere. It's incredibly soothing and arousing at the same time. Men seem inclined, however, to concentrate on tiny areas in a strict order – left nipple first, then right nipple, clitoris – and then they can clamber on top.

We have to show them there's more to it than that and the best way is simply with words: talk to him. For example, try saying, 'God, the small of my back is so sensitive – a man who strokes me there can do anything with me.' And then, when he does it, we can do all the back-arching and the 'Mmmm,

lovely,' and 'You're so good at this. Do it in little smooth circles with your fingertips, now up a bit towards the nape of my neck. Ooh, mmmm, no, not down there yet; it's too good, mmmm, yesss! …' And pretty soon it will be 'Ooh, mmmm.' That's unless he's a complete klutz, in which case, leave him – well, unless he's your husband or long-term partner, in which case, keep up the training.

> Touching – everywhere – is one of the great pleasures of sexual intimacy.

If you show your man how good it makes you feel – and if you return the compliment – he will soon take the first step towards becoming a great lover, which is learning that there's much, much more to sex than straight penetration.

The trouble is that far too many men don't understand that we naturally recoil from having living things suddenly plunged into our mouths. The best way to train them is to say, 'No, let me do it to you.' Then, kneeling over him, naked (this will engage his attention, you bet), just hold his head and kiss him as you would like to be kissed yourself.

kissing

'The one thing I hate,' said a friend, 'is the slab-of-condemned-veal stunt, where they go to kiss you and this great lump of flaccid meat just sort of flops into your mouth and hangs there.' 'I disagree,' said another. 'It's the Mad Rat that I can't stand, when this thing is writhing and squirming in a total frenzy, trying to get down your throat and kill you.'

Both these men definitely require training: you, the woman, just have to take control, saying, 'Here, let me do it to you.' And then, you must kiss him as you would like to be kissed. He'll get the point soon, particularly if you guide his hand downwards and say, 'See? How wet?' Reward, you see.

If it's someone you don't know that well, you might need to play it more subtly, but the principle is the same: show him what you want and reward him when he gives it to you. And if he does start the old condemned-veal routine, simply push his head back gently, gaze into his eyes and give him one of those sensual little cat-licks you'd like him to give to you. He'll soon get the point.

masturbating

You are a lucky, lucky woman if you have found a man who knows how to bring you to a climax with his fingers. Most of them are – and I say this without bitterness or resentment – hopeless. I have to say it in this way because, actually, most women are hopeless, too. When pressed, close male friends have revealed that we subject our men to a sort of all-out assault – as if we're trying to pump out a leaky boat. Both men and women could benefit from using 'Show And Tell' as a technique here. Let him watch you: it'll turn him on wildly and you will reveal lots of useful information at the same time.

Do you touch your clitoris directly, or off to one side? Do you stroke and caress your lips? Do you move in a circular, or side-to-side motion? As you get near the edge, do you speed up or slow down? Do you like to slip a finger – or something more – inside? Do you find that you like to close or open your legs as you get nearer? After all, he can't be expected to know all these things instinctively.

Even with such scant – though very graphic and practical – instruction, you'll find that you won't need to talk much when it comes to your lover's turn to try his hand, as it were. All you will need are a few simple, well-chosen commands (see Training your man, page 60) and you'll be able to get anything you want from him.

You will have to trust me when I say that this technique really does work beautifully. Do, please, though (for your own sake), resist the temptation to cry, 'Yes! YES! Good dog!' at the end.

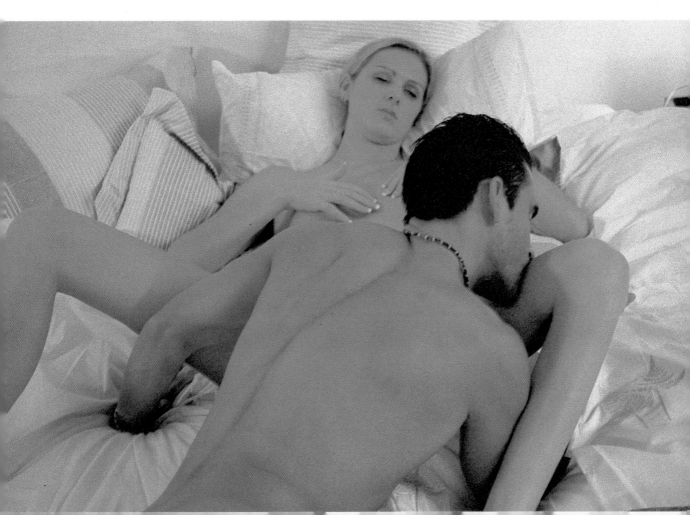

- The Labrador: endless pointless slobbering in the wrong place.
- The Dick Head: the man who mistakes his tongue for his penis and tries to shove it all the way in.
- The Rhythm King: the man who thinks that changing the rhythm every ten seconds is the key to being a good lover.
- The Karaoke Artist: the man who has once been told that if you hum against a woman's pussy it can feel pretty good, but hasn't realized that mumbling 'Strangers in the Night' and more *Best of Frank Sinatra* isn't quite what they meant.

oral sex

A good enough rule for being a Boudoir Goddess is, 'Never do with your hands what you could do with your mouth,' – and this applies to men as much as to women. Not every woman enjoys oral sex – 'I get lonely,' says one woman – but most of us do, and most of us would like more and better oral sex. But at some time or another, we've all had the 'Bad Oral Sex Experience' in one of its many guises:

- The Daring Vicar: a breath-held, tentative lick before he comes to the surface gasping.
- The North Sea Diver: the man who can hold his breath for ever but is just groping in the dark while he's down there.

As I've said before, a few well-chosen, very clear words and phrases plus feedback, whether verbal – 'Oh, that feels so good, there … yes, there!' – or physical – clutching his head or bucking your hips – will solve the problem. Slipping a finger down to help can also be very arousing for both of you – but it can also be disastrous: beware of the man who thinks, by doing this, you're really accusing him of being incompetent.

Try saying 'Oh darling, it's so good I can't help myself.' Men have such fragile egos really.

taking his time

This is the most important lesson for good lovers to learn and, it has to be said, if you don't want him to take his time – if you don't want the whole thing to last for a delicious, sensual eternity – you're probably with the wrong man. (If some of you *are*, and him taking more time is more than flesh can stand, then skip this bit and turn instead, to Spice it up, page 72, which is all about refreshing a tired relationship.)

Once you have trained him to take his time, whether it's by undressing slowly, piece by piece, or by pushing him away gently when he's rushing ahead and instead, turning your attentions to him, or just by using words, 'Oh, I love it when you just stroke me there really slowly,' and rewards, such as 'God, I am *so* turned on by you,' you must beware. There are some guys who think that this means you never want a fast, rough, no-messing quickie.

In short, be explicit about what you want him to do, reward him with your pleasure when he does it, and things will just get better and better between you.

Fun and games

WELL, IT'S all fun and games, really, isn't it? It certainly should be, but I have to admit it's pretty easy for sex – particularly long-term sex – to get one wheel in the sand (see Repetitive sex syndrome, page 75.) You know what I mean: emotionally it's fine – intimate, comfy, cosy – and physically, it ... *well*, it does the trick. But in terms of real sexiness or sensuality, it's just same old, same old stuff.

There's no need to go mad, though, splashing out millions on tropical island holidays or cruises through the Norwegian fjords; no need to hole up in a rented castle playing 'Madonna and the Entire Cast of *Sex*'. There are sexual and sensual diversions all around you, and how much better to cast a wicked new light on something familiar than to struggle with the plain brown wrapper of a mail-order sex gizmo while your man stands over you, squiggling with excitement, 'What is it? What is it? Is it something for the car? Is it ... oh.' 'Yes, it's a sou'wester [waterproof] and a whalebone leg. We're playing *Moby Dick* tonight.'

So, here, then, are a few simpler, and probably more gratifying, suggestions for you to ponder.

food

We take food for granted but how much seduction happens across the dinner table? The link between food and sex is too ancient to need restating.

Some foods are just plain sexy – try eating buttery asparagus, oysters, corn-on-the-cob; even the plain old banana can be a suggestive feast in the right hands and mouth. Some foods are sexy because of what they suggest. One of the raunchiest scenes ever is in Paul Pickering's novel *The Blue Gate of Babylon*, where two men and a woman eat almost-raw beefsteaks naked, the juices and blood running down their flesh ...

Feeding each other can be wildly sexy. Even the rather hackneyed old trick of eating food off your lover's body can be a turn-on if no one giggles. (A friend's fantasy, here, is, '... to be the table at a dinner. The food is laid out on me and all the men – it's only men, *elegant* men in dinner jackets – pick the food from my flesh with their fingers and finally, at the end of the meal, they turn their attentions to me.')

Just think of the words 'hot', 'moist', 'sweet', 'dripping' and the senses 'touch', 'taste', 'smell', and you'll get the point.

There are two things to say at this stage: first, forget table manners; use fingers and tongues. And second, never mind clearing up; it's going to be messy. Don't worry about that now – some things can wait until morning.

drink

Here's a little trick that will drive any man wild with desire for you. Take a sip of wine, hold it in your mouth, look him full in the eye, and then let it trickle slowly out of your mouth and down your chin as you run your tongue around your lips. Practise in the mirror first. Why it should turn them on so much, I don't know. (Actually, I *do* know, and so do you.)

Sweet wine passed from your mouth to his: that's a turn-on. A mouthful of hot coffee or cold iced water taken before you engulf him with your mouth: that's a turn-on. Anything that tells him you understand the connection between food and sex is a turn-on, and if you have an appetite for one, he'll be even keener to satisfy your taste for the other.

clothes

Yes, yes, I *know* we fought for generations for the right not to doll up like little playthings for the pleasure of men, but what we're aiming for here is a situation

where his pleasure is our pleasure, too. So think frills, silks, lingerie, lace, stockings, corsets. Corsets, as it happens, are a high-fashion item. Every home should have one, even if you don't have a man.

The truth is that many men do get excited by the combination of silk underwear and black stockings. While this makes our life much easier, it's not the only thing that works. What *always* works is the hint of the forbidden. Meet him for a drink and then, as mentioned earlier, tell him oh-so-casually that you're not wearing underwear. He is guaranteed to go wild, and he'll think you're the most adorable sex goddess on the planet.

Even your ordinary clothes can be a turn-on. Why? Because *you're* inside them, and *you're* what he wants. Can he have you? Sure he can. But make him wait. Undress with tantalizing slowness; get him to sit in a chair while you strip off in front of him – no touching. (Encourage him to take you to a table-dancing club to see how the professionals do it.) Embarrassed? Don't be – he'll be thrilled.

As for sex, remember that even a little scrap of something – a silk scarf, a feather boa, a thong, a ribbon – is always sexier than nothing at all. Why? Because it acts as a focus to draw the eye to the nakedness of the rest of you, and he'll love it.

the frugal sensualist

We're moving into the age of the designer sex toy: the £1,500 glass dildo, to name but one. The frugal sensualist can achieve similar effects, however, with readily obtainable household objects. A straw poll of women friends revealed precious few things around the house that haven't at one time or another been pressed into erotic service. Here's a selection to fire your imagination:

- Certain shampoo bottles – the design can't have been an accident, surely?
- Feathers – stroke with them for sensuality, tickle for wildness. (Remember the old definition. 'Erotic' is something you do with a feather; 'pornography' is something you do with a chicken.)
- Look in the fridge. Ice cubes. Make sure that they

are melting, and then hold them in your mouth and lick his nipples with your frozen tongue, go down on him with your Snow Queen mouth, pop one up his butt as he comes – or get him to do the same for you. Close his eyes and draw patterns on his skin with them.

- Ice cubes again. To be really provocative and if you have an open fire, heat a poker, show it to him, and then blindfold him. Bring it close to his skin so that he can feel the warmth, then put the poker away safely, and touch his flesh firmly with a melting ice cube. The skin can't immediately distinguish between cold and heat: Aieee! Then undo the blindfold for some passionate relief.
- Frozen peas. Wrap them around his cock and balls for a few seconds and then massage them back to warmth.
- Ice again. This time, hold a melting cube against his nipple for a few seconds then reheat it with your warm breath.
- Whipped cream slathered wherever you'd like to slather it, and licked off however you like.
- Check out that fruit bowl again (except the pineapples) and use your imagination.
- Scratch his skin oh so gently – with the tines of a fork, or sandpaper or a nail brush. But alternate the 'pain' with the pleasure of playful little licks and caresses.
- Ask him to bring you your shampoo bottle from the bathroom. Look him in the eye while you act out a scene from your imagination.
- Strip, straddle a kitchen chair like a cowgirl and challenge him to make you come.

And so on … The list is endless. Next time you go through the kitchen, keep your eyes open for the possibilities. You'll surprise yourself – and him. Just one thing: not the vacuum cleaner – *really*.

There are no possibilities in the vacuum cleaner. The tumble dryer … that's another story.

Spice it up

monogamy = monotony?

It's close – there are only three letters between them. Does being monogamous have to get monotonous? No, but let's be honest, despite the fact that on average married people have *more* sex than single people, you're unlikely to reach a double-figured anniversary without at least one long stretch where one or both of you lose interest in sex. It's impossible to maintain the same intense passion and frequency of sexual activity you knew at the start – you'd be physically and emotionally exhausted after a few months of weekends in bed and three-times-a-night sex. Unless, that is, you have absolutely nothing else to do. Of course, in those early days you tell yourself that you're going to be the only couple in history who will never tire of sex with each other because it's just *so* good.

But here's how it is: love and intimacy eventually replace feelings of lust and raw passion. You may still find each other hugely attractive but you start to find space in your relationship for the demands of real life. Work, friends and family begin to reclaim some of your attention. (This is often a huge relief to those around you. One of the world's greatest lies is, 'All the world loves a lover'.)

Even so, a call from him is still the highlight of your working day. You smile and think life is sweet, and sometimes just one look (*that* look) from him will make your heart lurch a little as it did in the early days. However, many couples discover even this blissful second stage wears off rather too rapidly.

A recent survey showed that after just *one year* of marriage most couples start saying 'no' to sex.

So what goes wrong? Is it the state of being married that makes a difference? Probably not, as we all know cohabiting couples who joke about their non-existent sex life. However, marriage does make sex legitimate and respectable, two words that tend not to evoke erotic responses in your brain. Could it be that once married, both men and women don't feel they have to make the effort to please/pleasure their partner in a sexual way? No one means to get complacent but you do get comfortable, rather too relaxed and used to each other. You're friends, hopefully, but you don't feel you have to make an effort to 'win' the other person: you already have them, lock, stock and in your living room – you only have to look at long-term couples you know to see it happening.

In the early days of wild sexual abandon, one couple I know hopped on trains and planes to attend orgies and couple-swapping parties.

Now, six years later, they fall into a shared bed in a shared house, often at different times, her with a mug of cocoa and him with a good book. Another couple I know quite well, who have lived together for 15 years, have sex about once a month. A pretty 33-year-old woman who'd lived with the same man for eight years said, 'We're good friends, we get on, but we just don't seem to have sex any more.'

Some people let work dominate their lives and, yes, it is hard in this day and age to keep a balance. One married woman friend in a high-powered job used to stagger home from her office so exhausted that she could barely speak for the first half an hour or so. Her one fantasy, she said, was to crawl in between white linen sheets on a comfortable bed and sleep. 'Any sexual move he made towards me I regarded as an affront,' she said. When the marriage took a turn for the worse, it needed a psychiatrist to point out that sex is part of the creative drive and all her client's 'creative drive' was being poured into her job. Exhaustion certainly does kill desire, but there are other reasons for loss of libido apart from the physiological, medical or hormonal ones.

If you're feeling used, unequal, angry or hurt on a regular basis, your desire to have sex with your partner can simply vanish. All too often, taking each other for granted leads to sexual indifference, not to mention the fact that the mundane nature of daily life can, let's face it, take its toll on the two of you as well. Romantic souls often find that living together, being too familiar, with no build-up of tension, ruins romance in the long term, which in turn ruins their sex life. Also, when sex is available night after night, it's easy to turn your back on it and leave it until another time. Sometimes the less you have, the less you want: you get out of the habit of making love.

Once your sex life starts to settle into a pattern, any differences in basic sex drive can also seem like loss of desire. If he's a twice-a-day man and you're a once-a-day woman at heart, your differences will be masked during the initial lusty, can't-keep-your-hands-off-each-other stage. A few months later, however, when your body starts to settle down and adopt its normal profile again, it will seem as though your libido has taken a dive.

Many women find that their body image and sexual self-esteem reduces with time and age – they just don't *feel* sexy or sexually attractive any more. During those *female* phone calls, women say to their friends: 'I look awful, I'm fat, my hair's a mess, I'm getting older.' I met one such woman friend for dinner recently. She has three children but she's roughly the same weight as she was before them; she has the same shiny, swingy hair, the same animated good-looking face, the same big eyes and wicked smile that I remember. Two men looked up at her as she walked through the restaurant. All that has changed is her confidence. Her husband is now running the large engineering company where he has worked for years. He puts in very long hours

and is rather too busy to stop and compliment her, to chat about her day with her, let alone help with the children's homework. 'I suppose we love each other,' she said. 'We just don't show it. I feel like a domestic blob, I never feel sexy. We only have sex occasionally.' Of course couples grow less intimate when communication channels break down and, as

The most *frequent* complaint from women is that sex becomes too routine and unexciting

has been previously said, it is natural for you not to want to have sex with someone who seemed distant and uncaring only a few hours before.

Mothers point out that sex goes out of the window immediately after childbirth when it's hard to re-establish a great sex life, though mainly because of exhaustion and lack of opportunity (see pages 84–5). Some couples realize that after the frantic sexual chemistry wears off, they are, in fact, rather incompatible. Similarly, a sagging sex life is often a symptom of a non-viable relationship, when lack of desire actually stems from a lack of love. The most *common* complaint from women, however, is that sex becomes too routine and unexciting.

repetitive sex syndrome

Everyone has comfort zones – habits and routines that you gradually adopt or fall into. You can spot your own by noticing any discomfort you may feel when you're asked to step outside them and do something different. Getting off the sofa and going to the gym for the first time is leaving a comfort zone, as is having to dress smartly to go to a party when you 'always' wear casual clothes. Whether you're asked to take on a new responsibility at work, or change the route you always take to get there, you'll find that some habits may have become a little too ingrained and cosy.

The same thing can happen with sex. Maybe you only have sex in your big comfortable bed? Perhaps Sunday morning is your regular slot? You've noticed how he always goes on top these days? Has foreplay become formulaic? Does sex always last the same length of time? These are all sexual comfort zones and they need to be thought about. If they become boring old routines, then the sex itself will become boring old sex and you'll be a victim of 'Repetitive sex syndrome'.

While it's not difficult to break out of your comfort zones, you do have to recognize and acknowledge them, and you need to *want* to break the monotonous pattern. It takes both courage and willpower to spice up your sex life: *you have to want to change your sexual pattern.*

starting over

Think sexy, think horny, think, 'I have a man and I deserve a great sex life.' Indeed, you both deserve a great sex life. You could mention this over the most intimate dinner you can arrange. Go out, stay in, but make sure it's reasonably romantic and you're looking good and wearing what you'd wear for a relaxed but sensual date. To show you mean business, then, you could initiate sex. Start with the obvious, such as experimenting with a new position together, or maybe try a different location. You could try more subtle changes, such as sex by candlelight, to music or while fully clothed. Imagine this is your first time with him. Think of the kind of tricks you might pull out of the bag and how flirtatious and sexy you'd be – or were – and can *still* be. Go back and read Chapter 2: Getting Down to It, page 24. Seize the moment. Get down to it.

Here are some other ideas to get you going:

1 Go to your local bookstore and browse through or buy some sex manuals. They're inspirational, full of useful hints and they might give you the push you need to try something new. For some of the best books, see page 122.

2 Read this book and watch the accompanying video with him. Suggest that you try some of the positions in these pictures.

3 Rifle through top-shelf magazines and see what other women get up to – women can often get turned on by looking at each other. And think, 'I could do that'. You probably can.

4 Watch a sexy movie or soft-porn video together.

5 Read through the sexiest scene in one of your favourite novels – aloud, perhaps – or even try a Black Lace book of your choice.

6 Tell him that you are a young virgin and he will have to seduce you before you will succumb. (See Fantasies, page 92.)

7 Give each other a slow, sensual massage.

8 Masturbate – but stop before you orgasm.

9 Close your eyes and conjure up some sexual images in your mind that you find really thrilling. Many women do this; it's not cheating at all.

10 Ask him how much he'd pay to have sex with you and take the money.

11 Suggest a period of enforced celibacy, the exact length of time to be decided, but possibly a week or two. During this time you should both behave as flirtatiously as possible towards each other. And although you may sleep in the same bed, and you may hug and cuddle, you should not have sex until the appointed day.

12 Masturbate at least once in the morning and once in the evening before the Great Sex Day, so you're truly in the mood.

13 Ask those women friends you consider still sexually very active to tell you about the most mind-blowing things they do during sex.

14 If you're not taking any exercise, start now. You'll soon feel better about yourself.

15 If all else fails, you may need a new lover. Affairs can often plug up the holes in marriages and long-term relationships. Not only do they add tension, drama and spice, they do reawaken dulled libidos. Then smuggle what you've learned, together with your new-found sexual zest, back into the main relationship. Of course it's a risk, but spending years in stultifying coupledom is no way to lead your life. If you really don't want to take a lover, act as if you have one anyway. Dress, think, act, flirt and play as if you're having an affair.

a word on locations

Sex in bed is comfortable, but sex in other places can sometimes be a very good idea, too. Some people make a hobby out of sex in unusual places. Everyone's heard of the mile-high club but there's also a below-sea-level club, a Euro Tunnel (or any other tunnel) club and a double-decker/Greyhound bus club. I've known people who've made out in Harrods, in Saks Fifth Avenue, on a fire escape and in a hospital, but there's no need to go that far unless you insist. Having sex on the sofa at home because you're too horny to get up and go to bed will do for starters. When was the last time you hopped into the shower or bath together, or had

sex in the sea or in a private pool? Has it occurred to you to park in a quiet street on the way home from an evening out and fool around in the car?

Lots of people like sex outside, whether it's under the stars or warmed by the sun on a summer's day.

You could wear your sexiest bra and pants, plan a meal outside and make a lazy sexy day of it. Is there a nude beach near you with somewhere you can play in private, perhaps? You may not have to go any further than your own garden, if you have one.

The prospect of sex in public or semi-public places is appealing for many people who like the added excitement of the risk of getting caught. Whether it's a quickie in the bathroom at a party, or up against a wall in a hotel corridor, why should you leave the fun of semi-public sex to couples who've only just met?

Part of the thrill is the sheer urgency of it. It's fast because you really don't want to be caught in the act; it's super-sexy because you want each other so badly you can't wait any longer. 'At least we *tried*,' said a friend of mine when coitus was interruptus – by a man and his dog, which was barking furiously as she and her husband humped away happily in the sand dunes in East Hampton. It's deliciously easy because you know each other well, and if it all goes wrong, you can laugh about it later on when you finally climb into the comfort of your double bed.

Back in the saddle

LOVE AFFAIRS END. The-too-hot-not–to-cool-down ones, and the ones that became a habit because they were good sex and pleasant company, and some weekends you thought, 'Maybe this is as good as it gets.' Then there's the man you were finally convinced was the real thing, and he wasn't. He's the one you don't recover from for ages. When you eventually crawl back to yourself again and start liking life as a free woman, the last thing you want to do, you tell all your friends, is 'get involved again'. What such a statement often means is, 'I'm not desperate. I'm functioning pretty well on my own and I'm certainly *not* up for any more pain and aggravation at the moment. Of course, though, if someone adorable should come along, that would be lovely – but I'm not looking.'

Marriages do end. The average marriage in the UK lasts nine years. Divorce is said to rival death and road accidents as a major cause of depression. It's bad enough breaking up when you're dating or living together but, whatever the reason, with divorce there's often a sense of failure. 'I've been married twice and failed both times,' groaned Joan Bakewell (60-something TV broadcaster) recently. Yet others might see elegant and intelligent Ms Bakewell's personal life as two relationships that ran their course. Today you don't *have* to stay until the bitter end. Fewer people are willing to do so. Social and religious pressures, such as they are in Western society, aren't enough to make unhappy couples stay together. In fact, nearly 50 per cent of divorces occur by the eighth year of marriage. While this may be tough on any children, it's not nearly as bad for them as staying with two openly hostile parents.

One woman I know insists that good marriages make good divorces. If the two of you can face up to the fact that, even though you like each other, the marriage is over, then you can have an amicable divorce. 'After initial sadness and feeling lonely, you do eventually meet someone else,' she said. 'No one wants a marriage to end, but sometimes they do. You're bored, you've outgrown each other … But if you're decent people, you wish each other well in the future; you try to stay friends if there are children involved; and you get on with your life. If there's a ton of bitterness and resentment, it's harder to get involved with someone else. God knows, in the early post-divorce days, you're not exactly a bundle of confidence, but that comes with time. You start flexing your "single" muscles again.'

But if you think you've 'failed' and you see yourself as a bad risk, if the marriage ended badly, if you were the injured party, or if you've been with the same partner for many years, it can take real courage to try again.

'I don't know if I can trust anyone now, or if I can be bothered with men,' said one woman whose husband had affairs, some of which she knew about at the time and others which she discovered after the divorce. One sweet-faced, blonde 37-year-old friend, who's been with the same man for 19 years, said, 'Getting divorced is my idea. I've known for ages that he isn't right and I feel OK. I've made the right decision. But I just dread starting again. I'm fine with women friends, going to restaurants, going on holiday and being flirty, but I've got absolutely *no* confidence about sex.'

Lots of women drift into involuntary celibacy. It isn't a conscious choice, it isn't an avowed anti-man stance, or some religious decision. Sometimes it happens. You think, 'OK, I'll do something else, I'll take a break.' You can't live without air and water; you can live without sex.

I remember a conversation when a gang of close-knit work colleagues owned up to no sex for periods of between six months and three years. When we discussed why 'women like us' should be living like this, we thought we'd outgrown mere sexual curiosity. We were too grown-up and independent for silly compromises and we certainly

didn't need a man to make our life work, although one of us *had* been tempted: 'But then I thought, "I'm not in the mood" and didn't ring back,' she said.

One of us had survived a serious illness. 'You know, when you're thinking about just staying healthy and getting a job again, sex just isn't high on your priority list,' she said. As we were the sort of friends who were brutally honest, we said probably we felt scared, self-protective. We'd all been hurt, if not the last time then the one before. 'I think I've forgotten how to do it,' said the single parent among us. The rest of us nodded, or drew in our breath.

Yet the joy and wonder of love, romance and sex is that it can happen again – at any time. No matter how bad or difficult your past has been, no matter how much you vowed, 'never, *ever* again', time heals. Memories fade. Provided you learned something from your experiences, provided you aren't firmly and irrevocably closed to the idea of falling in love again, of having a sexual relationship again, you *can* do it. When the timing is right and the man is right, you seem to know it instinctively. Sometimes you realize, in retrospect, that the break, the celibate time, has been good for you.

A busy architect friend, whose husband had died, said, 'I suppose it takes as long as it takes to meet the next right man. I'd sort of forgotten about it – given up, you might say. Then this man and I met briefly and I felt hugely attracted to him. It was an extraordinary feeling after all that time. There was a series of increasingly erotic e-mails. Then he came to stay. Of course it crossed my mind that it had been ten years since I'd had sex with anyone and I wondered what it would be like, and if I'd be any good, but it was electric. All I'd forgotten was how good sex could be.' They plan to live together very shortly.

Another friend – the kind of woman who makes men sigh – was reminiscing about the agony and sweetness of getting back in the saddle. 'I know how to look pretty,' she said. 'But deep down, I'm small-town shy and I always have been. After my divorce, I was just hopeless. Yes, I went out with men but I didn't even ask them back for a drink. I was accused of being a bit cold, and I could see what someone might mean. But I was just plain terrified and very rigid. I thought, men might get the wrong idea if I was warmer, and I wouldn't have known what to do. I wore too much make-up; my clothes were much too smart for the cinema and the local Italian place. The cushions on my sofa were plumped up like helium balloons and I jumped if a man put his hand on my arm in the car. Oh God, how did I get through that bit of life being so uptight?'

She continued, 'And then along came Charlie. He's younger than me, not great-looking, but the kindest, most relaxed man in the world. He ignored all my coolness and didn't rush me; just kept asking me out. You know, to the theatre, a concert, once for fish and chips with friends. He did say then, "Wear jeans – I bet you look wonderful in jeans." So I wore jeans. He offered to cook for me because he said he was a brilliant cook – which he is. Never even tried to kiss me good night. It took me six months to go to bed with him because it took me that long to relax, unwind. But by then I was starting to find him sexually attractive. When, finally, I did get round to climbing into bed with him one Saturday evening, you know, it was just so easy, so natural. That old Barbra Streisand song, "Ain't love easy?" flashed through my mind.'

I empathized with her. I'd had a dry spell that lasted for two years. I *definitely* wasn't looking. But on the first evening of four days on a Mediterranean island I met a man with thick, shiny dark brown hair, impeccable manners, wicked eyes and a deep voice, and I was stirred. We saw each other for three days – I could scarcely sleep; I couldn't believe that, out of the blue, I was finding a man so amazingly sexual. On the third night I went to bed with him. Not my style, but 'life's short' and, yes, it was delicious.

What has since struck me, because that was nine years ago and we are still very good friends, is that if it's right, it's dead simple – and hideously exciting. There's no time to fret and worry; you don't forget how to do sex. You just *do* it. It's nice if you can plan divine underwear … it's not necessary. But never try the starting-over routine out of desperation. Any fool can do that; and lots do. It just doesn't work. But many women say that back-in-the-saddle sex is the nicest, sweetest, most meaningful and even, sometimes, the most enthralling sex of their lives.

'… like not realizing you're hungry or even wondering if you should eat, and then someone places before you the most fabulous French food. Of course you say, "yes"; of course you realize how hungry you were. "And it is so worth the wait," you think, as you lick your lips and smile.'

Sex in pregnancy

SO, RECREATIONAL sex became procreational sex and now you're having a baby. Will it affect your sex life? Are you *kidding*? It will never be quite the same again. First, you have the nine months' waiting time to get through and however thrilled you are, you do look – and feel – like a stranded whale. Then there's the post-birth recovery period, when many women swear that they'll never have sex again if it means they might have to go through *that* again. Yet time heals.

To that, of course, you have to add another 18 years or so of minding the baby/child/teenager until she/he grows up, leaves home and leaves you both in peace. But that's the way most (though not all) of us want to – and choose to – live. And even from the other side (as parents), we wouldn't have it any other way and thank God our parents did it.

bedding Buddha

As we've seen throughout this book, when it comes to women and sex, there are no general rules. During pregnancy, this becomes even more apparent. Some women really do look, and feel, extraordinarily sexy when pregnant. Like fertility goddesses surging with hormones, they bloom. They can't get enough sex and are utterly turned on by their altered state. For others, sex is the last thing on their mind, at the bottom of a very long 'to do' list. One friend of mine said she couldn't stand the sight of herself, or her husband – 'I'm bloated, bad-tempered, and I don't have fingers any more: I have sausages.' Another said, 'I'm scared, tired, I snap at him and I wonder how he puts up with me. I can quite understand why some men go to prostitutes when their wives are pregnant.'

Some women adore their firm, swelling breasts and stomach, and marvel at nature's genius during every step of their pregnancy. Many men, too, are incredibly turned on. Others hate the pregnant state, from the 'putting-on-a-bit-of-weight' stage through the weeks until their lovers become fit to burst.

The first three months (or first trimester) – and longer if you're unlucky – is often characterized by chronic morning sickness, which can last all day long. And/or you may also experience a dragging tiredness, unlike anything you've ever known before. Not surprisingly, women who feel sick and tired all the time don't feel much like sex either. However, the middle three to six months see many women positively blooming, with their energy and libido back, and an 'I'm–up-for-it' look in their eyes again. At this point *some* women experience a huge surge in their sex drive; a few even say that they had the best sex of their lives during this stage of their pregnancy.

But it's also a time for marked mood swings. All those raised hormone levels cause your normal emotions to be heightened, so that you'll cry more easily, feel hurt unnecessarily and often feel quite soppy and sentimental. And what about the man involved – your partner? How's he feeling? He's in awe of what's happening to you and your body, and is often more solicitous than usual. He could even be wary of sex with you, however attractive he finds you; he's scared he may do some damage.

Men sometimes take a little while to adjust to impending fatherhood. Remember that he will see you differently now. Your changing shape – rounder, fuller, riper – indicates that you're, literally, becoming a mother figure. As you transform into a mother before his eyes, he may grieve that his sexy girlfriend has gone for ever. It can be hard for men (and women, too) to equate 'sex' with 'motherhood'. You'll be relieved, however, to know that these feelings pass.

As you become the star of the show, some men can get jealous – he may remind people, 'It's my baby, too.' And it may begin to dawn on him that he might have to sacrifice his sex life, as he knows it, for this unborn child. No wonder nature designed human pregnancies to last nine months – you both need at least that long to adjust.

Most men will want to take their cue from you about whether to have sex and, if so, how, when and where. Here are some common concerns:

How can he possibly fancy me when I look like this?

In fact, to many men their pregnant partner is sexier than ever: you even smell sexier. And you're going through something wonderful together. If you look in the mirror and shudder, remember that you're not going to look like this for ever. And your body is performing a miracle: by growing a baby, and its life-support system, inside you. With nature's help, you and your man have created another person whom you'll both love for the rest of your lives.

Is it safe to have sex? Can he hurt the baby?

'Normal' sex is completely safe at any time during a normal pregnancy (unless your obstetrician advises otherwise). However, this is not the time

for you to be experimental. Avoid anything that could damage your cervix or introduce an infection. Clean fingers and penises are fine – don't try anything else. He cannot hurt you or the baby with his penis. However, you may find your preferences change. You might want to go slower; you might want deeper penetration (or shallower); you might want his penis to hit a different spot. So show him, explain to him.

Women who've had a previous miscarriage *may* be advised to abstain from sex for the first three or four months of pregnancy, but even in women predisposed to miscarriage, there is no evidence at all that sex can cause one.

Women suffering from one fairly rare condition, called placenta previa, should *not* have intercourse because their placenta has attached in too low a position by the cervix. There are other good reasons not to have sex: if you experience any vaginal bleeding, say, or if your 'waters' have broken. If you are in any doubt, check with your doctor.

Can the baby hear or feel you having sex?

The foetus's ears are fully formed and operational by five months. So, when you're halfway through your pregnancy the foetus can probably hear your voices, screams and moans. She/he will also be able to feel the ripples of an orgasm. So, mother and father have sex? It's normal: it sounds as if you love each other.

Can sex, especially an orgasm, bring on labour?
Yes, and no. Not unless you're about to go into labour anyway, but in that case, yes. I've known many women have sex in an attempt to start labour when they're overdue. This works on two levels, supposedly: your own orgasm will start moving the right muscles, and the prostaglandins in sperm – orally or vaginally – can help the final ripening of the cervix. Sex can kick-start labour then, *if* – and only *if* – you were only hours away from labour anyway.

How do you get near enough to each other to have penetrative sex, but avoid squashing the baby?
You're right … the missionary position is not the best idea, and anyway, once your stomach becomes a huge, swollen bulge, it's almost impossible to achieve. (See Six ways to have sex, pages 41–53.) The rear entry position, where your bump is pointed away from all the action, feels

pretty good. You could also try 'spoons' for a loving, cuddling sex session; or get on top, kneeling over him, facing whichever way you choose, with him putting his hands on your hips to help move the extra weight. Or, you could lie back on the edge of the bed while he stands or kneels in front of you, depending on the height of your bed.

Should we use a condom?
One of the big bonuses of being pregnant is that you don't have to worry about birth control for the duration, so enjoy it while it lasts. Incidentally, a man's ejaculate cannot enter the womb because your cervix is sealed off with a mucous plug until labour commences.

sex after childbirth

There *are* women who resume their sex life almost immediately. These are incredibly lucky women who probably gave birth with just a few moans and shudders, and definitely no stitches. *Most* women, however, suffer some degree of 'trauma' to their vagina and perineum during childbirth. This could include tears/cuts and consequent stitches, as well as bruising and swelling. Generally, you are advised to wait until after the six-week doctor's check-up before resuming sex. Even those who have a Caesarian section, for whom there is no vaginal discomfort, may find it takes a few weeks for the abdominal scar to heal and for sex to feel comfortable.

First-time-afterwards sex does tend to make you feel rather anxious. You may hear horror stories from mothers who complain that they were not sewn up the same as before, or tales of doctors who like to think they have made women a little tighter.

Then you hear men complaining that sex after childbirth is like 'waving your willy in a wellie'. Combine this with general postnatal tenderness and extreme tiredness, and you can understand why new mothers worry about having intercourse. Some women say it's almost like being a virgin – *you* worry *it* might hurt; *he* worries *he* might hurt you. You want to do it and you want to put the first time behind you, but you're still scared of doing it.

The virginity analogy is probably a good one to keep in mind. Tell him how you feel and what you're scared of. Just go slowly: you don't have to have intercourse until you feel more confident. Have lots of non-penetrative sex first. Then, when it feels right and you're ready, go for the slowest, gentlest sex

session possible. Even if you just know that he will stop in a nano-second if you say so, you'll feel better. And, by the way, it *will* be OK. A few weeks on and you'll wonder what you were making all the fuss about. By then your main problem will be finding the time and opportunity to have sex, not to mention trying to summon up the energy.

post-baby body

So, is your body different after giving birth? Having a baby causes your kidneys to grow, your heart to enlarge and your lower ribs to flare out. Your pelvic girdle also extends to accommodate your growing baby and it may take two years for your pelvis to return to its previous dimensions. There are also changes to the front of your pelvic girdle, the symphis pubis, which are permanent.

your vagina

After what seems like the longest and heaviest period known to woman, the bleeding gradually stops, any stitches are removed or melt away, and swelling and bruising eventually disappear. After about a month outward appearances seem normal again, but what about inside?

The vagina, which has stretched to allow your baby to be pushed through, reverts to its normal size quite quickly (so ignore all those willy-in-a-wellie stories). However, the vaginal walls do not return to normal for some time. They are thinner, the folds have gone and lubrication takes longer (and there is less of it).

For a while the intensity of your orgasms is also weaker. But after three months your vaginal folds are back, lubrication is normal and your orgasmic potential is huge once more.

therapy (HRT) can work miracles. HRT replaces the natural oestrogen in the female body with a synthetic version that's indistinguishable to the body from the real thing. The skin feels plumper; vaginal dryness goes away; hot flushes stop. Go on HRT early enough and your menopause may well pass unnoticed. (Unless you've had a hysterectomy, you will also be given progesterone to protect against possible cervical or uterine cancer later in life.) And the lawyer I mentioned? She went on HRT and within a couple of weeks was transformed: 'I feel younger, I *look* younger. I've got more energy and, best of all, my libido has come back. My husband thinks I'm up to something. Well, I *am* – but only with him,' she told me.

Yet, oddly enough, it's the *male* hormone testosterone, which can have the most dramatic effects. Testosterone levels, too, plummet in post-menopausal women and the effects can be general timidity, anxiety, an inability to confront the world (almost indistinguishable from depression), as well as diminished energy levels and a loss of sex drive. Testosterone implants, placed beneath the skin of the stomach, can reverse these changes. 'I just started feeling scared and weepy. Everything seemed such an effort, and I completely lost interest in sex,' said one glamorous, sexy academic friend with 'a Past', whose future seemed to have turned into a bit of a desert. 'Then I had a combined oestrogen/testosterone implant. I hadn't realized how far downhill I'd gone, but within two days my energy came surging back and with it, my sexuality. It's better now than it's ever been.'

Some women don't like (possibly, *don't approve of*) testosterone therapy. Feminist Germaine Greer once famously said that it made her understand how a rapist feels. But one of the great proponents, Professor John Studd, who pioneered HRT in the UK, is in no doubt. He compares the sadness, the nerves and the low-testosterone lack of energy of the more unlucky among menopausal women, with the symptoms of nineteenth-century mad women in the attic, shut away from family, friends, lovers and life. He says that although you can't *prove* how many of them simply had hormonal problems, he's absolutely sure it was a *huge* proportion of them.

The pros and cons of HRT have been well argued. On the plus side, there's clear evidence that HRT improves the memory; protects against osteoporosis; decreases hot flushes and insomnia; enhances the mood; and restores sexual and general energy levels. The down side, however, is that some women experience PMS (pre-menstrual syndrome) symptoms from the progesterone; there may possibly be an increased risk of uterine cancer; and some have associated HRT with breast cancer. To quote two clichés for the price of one: 'There's no such thing as a free lunch,' and 'You pays your money and you takes your choice.'

after the menopause

With, or without HRT – though it should be said, mostly *with* – many, many women report that the time after the menopause is the happiest of their whole lives. Freed from the monthly hormonal assault, they find a new sense of self-possession in every sphere of life. 'I've never felt more my own woman,' said one woman, a high achiever and a mother of three. 'I was expecting it to be hell, but apart from the hot flushes, which were a pain in the butt, its been easy. It's as though I've done my bit for Mother Nature and now I can do my bit for *myself*.' In her case, it's not sexuality but her passion for exotic, and often rough-shod, travel.

Another friend said, 'Sex? Never been better. I hadn't realized how much I was watching the calendar, thinking, "Is this the month the bloody Pill doesn't work?" That's done with now; it's just about pleasure and good loving. The only thing I *don't* have is firm flesh. But you know something? I've yet to meet a *man*, as opposed to some boy or gay fashionisto, who gives a flying fuck about firm flesh.'

And she's right, of course. She's got something better. Call it experience, call it confidence, call it style, intelligence, understanding (of herself *and* others): whatever you call it, it *works*. Menopause? Its just a phase you go through.

4

Getting Wilder

Fantasies

THE WORLD IS divided into two sorts of people: those who have sexual fantasies, and those who aren't telling the truth. The truth is that everyone has them. The Queen? You bet. Hillary Clinton? Of course she does. Well, there may be an exception that proves the rule.

> And as for men ... The things that go on in men's minds are almost as lurid as the things that go on in women's. You don't believe me? Read Nancy Friday's book *Men in Love* – and prepare to be astonished.

Sexual research shows that women who have a full fantasy life have better orgasms. There's another division, of course: between those fantasies which might, one day, if you're in the right mood and everything comes together (as it were), be acted out in reality, and those which should really, really be kept in your imagination as private treasures. You may decide that you want to share them with your partner, of course; both men and women report a huge buzz – not just of erotic excitement, but intimacy, too – when they share their very innermost sexual secrets.

Men love it because it shows them, as one man told me, '... that she's not just having sex to please me, as part of some trade-off, but she's really into it for herself, as well.' And we love it because, well, as a friend said, 'I've always had to keep my real sexuality under wraps. I always thought it would turn a man off if he knew I had an erotic imagination as graphic and as, well, lurid, as any man's. But my current partner is different. He encouraged me to talk about my fantasies and it's not just a huge turn-on, it's also a sort of relief. I mean, here's this man who knows the darkest depths of my erotic imagination, and he still adores me. It's thrilling.'

As another friend put it, 'I'm sure he'd rather know that I'm fantasizing about being carried out to some appalling workshop and being used as a plaything by three oily, rough truckers than suspect I'm thinking lovey-dovey thoughts about leaving him and setting up home with Gary from the office.'

the fantasy life

We all have a 'Secret Me'; if we didn't, we might well go crazy, and that secret life applies to sex as much as to anything else. Our 'Secret Me' looks different, *is* different, likes different things, lives somewhere else with someone else, has different experiences. The day we stop having a 'Secret Me' is the day we give up and settle down to wait for the end.

to act out or not to act out?

Some people will say, 'Never, *ever* act out your "Secret Me". At best, it will be a disappointment, at worst, a hideous embarrassment.' Others say, 'Go for it, whatever it is. You only live once and the only things you regret are the things you didn't do.'

Basically, there are four sorts of 'Secret Me' fantasies, and we all know (though we may well disagree) where each of them belong.

The four categories are:

- Things we'd love to act out and would do like a shot if the right moment came along.
- Things we might just do if the time was right and the mood was right, and we were with the right person and the music was right, and the lighting was right, and our stomachs were much flatter, and we a good deal thinner, especially our thighs.

The only truth about your 'Secret Me' is that she can be whatever you want; that's why they're called 'fantasies'.

- Things that we wouldn't mind watching and if everything was right (see above) we might just join in, but probably not.
- Things that are absolutely, definitely, permanently, no-question-about-it for the 'Secret Me' only – because we know damn well that in real life, rather than in the realms of the subconscious, they'd be dangerous or nasty, or 'icky' or illegal.

whatever you want

If you want the full skinny on the wild, wonderful (and sometimes downright weird) world of fantasy, take a look at any of Nancy Friday's books (or, if you're particularly lucky, just take a look – an *honest* look – inside your own head). Here, too, are a few women friends' favourite 'Secret Selves' revealed, as always, after a glass or two of Chardonnay.

pretty woman

You think men liked Julia Roberts (and her body double) in *Pretty Woman*? Well, women liked her, too – at least the women in this group of friends. They liked the idea of this rich, successful guy being weak at the knees for … well, for her flesh. It was pure sexual desire, so much so that he'd pay hard cash for her body. 'It's the anonymity,' said one. 'I think it must be really sexy to knock on that hotel door and not know who's going to be on the other side. And getting yourself ready, you know? Just like something expensive, in a shop, gift-wrapped.'

'I pretend I'm her,' said one woman. 'I often do. I can't imagine a woman who's never wondered what it must be like to go whoring. My boyfriend doesn't know, of course. He just thinks I'm really hot that night. I let him go to bed first. Then I come into the bedroom like it's a 6-star hotel and he's paid me, and then …

well, I just go to work on him with things I wouldn't do normally. But I'm this expensive hooker and so – this is the weird bit – it's like I have to do all this stuff to earn my £1,000, or whatever. And then I get really turned on, but I tell myself I mustn't come because that would be unprofessional … it's wild.'

the hunky repairman

We all know this one. It's one of the oldest staples of the porno movie. Bored housewife, broken washing machine, hunky repairman, slinky lingerie. 'Is there anything else I can help you with, madam?' Of course there is, and whereas, in real life, the repairman would have left his tool at home, this version never has. The repairman is always hunky, too, rather than the completely spherical, balding, harassed father-of-six real-life model, who seems not only to have a penchant for nylon shirts but a bit of an aroma problem, too.

Nevertheless, 'It's the power thing again,' said one friend. 'I mean, he knows he'll never get someone like me ... And I'm fresh out of the bath, smelling of perfume and I just open my heavy silk negligee and ... Actually, the other day the hose broke on the dishwasher and my guy said he could fix it. There he was, down there for ages with his Leatherman, grunting. I went up and had a bath and ... well, I expect you can guess the rest.'

underneath the lamplight

Here's another friend's ultimate favourite 'Secret Self': 'Nothing like *Pretty Woman*,' she says. 'Quite the opposite. I'm this really, *really* cheap, reluctant streetwalker. Common and tarty, a complete whore – short skirt, ripped fishnets, cheap stilettoes, with too much lipstick. These dreadful guys in company cars are kerb-crawling. I wiggle a bit, tilt my hip, give them the come-on. And of course in the fantasy I'm really bored as well. You know, just another punter. But I get in the car and they drive me to some really foul-smelling, filthy goods yard or something and just use me. My best one is when he's got me kneeling half-in, half-out of the car. My skirt's pulled up and he pulls my pants to one side ... they can never wait; they're just, you know, in and out. They just have me, there are no preliminaries or anything, it's just four or five thrusts and that's it. And then they're disgusted with themselves for sinking this low, and they just throw the money at me. It's really, *really* degrading; it's really, *really* sexy. Best of all, I enjoy every really, *really* thrilling minute.'

'I mean, he

knows he'll never

get someone

like me . . .'

father and son

'Oh, come on,' I said. 'No, no,' she said. 'Think about it. There you are with this gorgeous ATB, when . . .' 'What's an ATB?' I asked. 'An Almost-Toy-Boy,' she said. 'You know, young and good-looking and toned, and all those things, but there's some substance to him – I mean, he can talk and he can listen, and he's actually interested. Anyway, so you're back at his place, and you're just getting down and dirty when you hear a key turn in the lock and this man comes in. Older, but very, *very* sexy – you know, something commanding about him? And he's beautifully dressed, and that really sexy hair – thick, with grey wings, you know? And he says, "Oh, excuse me, I seem to be interrupting something here." But he doesn't go away. Instead, he says, "I must congratulate you, my boy, on your taste. She is exquisite," and he sits down beside you and kisses your hand. Then the ATB is kissing the side of your neck while his father is stroking you, and then . . .' 'Yes?' I asked. 'Oh, for heavens sake,' she said, 'Do I have to spell it out?'

all the nice girls love a sailor

There's something about men in uniform – the uniform, probably. But it can't just be the uniform or we'd all be hot for traffic wardens. It's the maleness of it, the hint of command and authority and discipline – the sense that, well, you'd be in safe hands, in every sense of the words.

One friend likes green: 'Green uniforms with lots of pockets and those brown leather belts with guns and things. It's a customs post somewhere remote and I don't speak the language, and they're suspicious. So they make me get out of the car and I'm only wearing this thin dress from Dolce & Gabbana or sometimes it's Betsey Johnson, but anyway . . . I'm very cold and it's windy up in the mountains – did I mention it was in the mountains? Well, it is – and they make me go into this little hut. And the commander one, who's a bit rough and unshaven, but big and strong, says he'll let me go if I please them – *all of them. I have to please the lot.* So there's this rough blanket . . .'

Another friend likes policemen. 'Are you mad?' I asked. 'Italian policemen,' she said, 'with those tight trousers with the red stripe, and their leather boots; that self-important swagger and the way they look at you with those big, brown eyes. I drive badly and jaywalk deliberately and things when I'm in Rome, so that they'll pull me over and take me up to the Castel St-Angelo, and lead me into this huge office with an enormous desk and then they say it will be easier for me if I talk, but . . .' *Mm-hmm.*

crossing the great divide

Over our third glass she said, 'I don't see why only blokes can be transvestites. Sometimes I think I'd like to dress up as a man', she continued, 'and just pick someone up, you know, at a bar or something. Then later on I'd guide his hand down my ...' 'He'd be gay,' I said. 'If you picked him up and he thought you were a man, he'd be gay.' 'Oh, for God's sake,' she said, 'This is a *fantasy*.'

Another friend fantasized about cross-dressing the other way round. 'I imagine this guy. He's a bit diffident', she said, 'and I encourage him to say what's on his mind. Eventually, he confesses that he's always wondered what it would be like to dress as a woman. So then I say, "Well, let's find out," and ...

'I put him in all the stuff – you know, lacy bra and stockings and silkies. And then I do the works make-up-wise, and then I say, "Now, you just lie back and let me take care of you. You be a good girl and you'll be very, very happy." And then you do it.' 'Do what?' I said. 'Absolutely everything you can think of that you'd like someone to do to you – in real life or in your fantasy world,' she replied.

I don't fancy mine much

'This body-fascism', said a friend, 'these designer gay boys – it's all rubbish. You know what I fantasize about? Uglies. Really ugly men. You know, you're in a taxi and the driver is fat, ugly and middle-aged and you can see him eyeing you up in the rear-view mirror and you know he is never, *ever* going to have anyone as gorgeous as you, and you almost want to say, "You want me? So, have me." He'd just be so thrilled and so grateful.'

'Sometimes I'll be walking along and there'll be these men – construction workers or truck drivers, or just ordinary, ugly, dud guys, boring men from boring offices walking along – and I'll think, "Hey, I could completely transform your life", just by walking up to them and offering to fuck them. It's as simple as that. "Hey, you want to fuck me?" There's nothing more to it. It must be a power thing. But I get so horny, just thinking about it. Uglies.'

Another rather well-endowed friend said she'd once sat in bed naked in a smart hotel in Madrid. She'd seen the ugly waiter and decided to order more room service. 'His eyes just came out on stalks as he walked in with this large tray and stared at me,' she said. 'I patted the bed and said, "Put the tray here," and I lightly rubbed my left breast. I felt sensationally sexy. He was powerless and I nearly had an orgasm.'

'And Fatties,' said another friend. 'I used to work with this man who was really fat. In fact, he was huge. He might have been an Ugly, too. But you couldn't tell because he had this fat-man face – you know, the way they just look like all the other fat men – and this great belly. But it all looked solid: every bit of him – not flabby. And I used to sit there looking at him and thinking, "God, imagine all that weight when it's thrusting; imagine the power." I'm sure he must have noticed that I was looking at him but he'd never have thought I was thinking about what it would be like to fuck him. I mean, no way would he assume. If only he knew ...'

If only they knew ... but that's the joy of the 'Secret Me'.

Fantasy – or reality

THE FANTASIES we've talked about so far are the ones probably best *not* put into practice. Not only because of what your dull cousin Enid told you: 'Best keep them as fantasies, sweetie; reality will only be a let-down.' Practically speaking, they also need clued-up accomplices who (a) know the script, and (b) will guarantee to stick to it. And that's not easy. As we all know, acting is best left to the professionals. It's all too easy for the rest of us to suddenly slip out of character and start giggling – and giggling and fantasy sex really *don't* mix.

The next few recipes for wildness, though, don't call for acting skills. Some, no doubt, will strike you as horrid/tasteless/inexplicable/ludicrous. Others ... well, let's just say they've all been suggested by women who've not just *thought* about them, but have actually *done* them, too: in many cases, repeatedly – *and* gleefully.

toy boys

One of the greatest benefits of getting a little older is that you can treat yourself to a toy boy. To some women, the idea is crazy; they like their man to be in control. But to others, the prospect of an energetic, compliant, youthful and, above all, *grateful* lover with bags of stamina and excitement ... well, it gives them quite a buzz. The toy boy is amazed and delighted with everything you do to him, or get him to do to you. Your sexual sophistication will obliterate any hankering he might have for the glossy mane and pert buns of girls who only have youth to offer. By the time you get into toy-boy territory, you'll know what you want and you'll know how to get it – something younger women simply haven't had time to find out. Yes, you'll probably have to make the first move, and it might have to be pretty unmistakable: think stocking tops, or perfumed breasts, think of running your hand 'accidentally' over the bulge in his pants while looking him full in the eye. He'll get the message. Sex with an older woman is one of the most popular fantasies among men, and if you're his best friend's mother, you have undoubtedly been the object of his desire for years.

> But remember: don't treat your toy boy like a man. He's not your equal, and *certainly* not superior to you.

This is one relationship where *you* are in control, and, as one long-term toy-boy enthusiast said, 'They'll leave you in the end, and always for someone younger than you. That's cool. What I do is give them one last night. I pull every trick out of the bag and by dawn they're *exhausted*, and I know full well that they're going to spend the rest of their life with pretty-but-dull little Twinky remembering it and wondering whether they did the right thing.'

threesomes

There are plenty of women who think two's company and three's a change. 'But where does everything *go*?' complained one friend, 'and do you take it in *turns*, or what?' 'Don't worry,' our adventurous friend said, 'it all happens naturally.' Two men, one women; two women, one man – either can be fun, although both have their drawbacks. If it's a two-man deal, they tend, being nervy creatures, to be wary and on edge in case they should, er, brush against something. Women don't have that problem, for whatever reason. So how do you go about it? It's not that difficult.

If it's two men plus you, then *you* make the running. If it's two women, then you and she collude, and he won't be able to believe his luck.

And the down side? 'I advertised,' says one friend, 'because I was curious. This really charming couple answered the ad and we met regularly for some months. It was, in purely sexual terms, the most erotic experience of my life. But then he fell in love with me – rang up, sent me notes. So I ended it. They're still together, I'm glad to say.'

moresomes

'Wife-swapping' has a hideous image and it's easy to see why. Ask a woman who tried it and *hated* it. 'For starters, you *never* find a couple who both of you want to make it with. And then what? Do you do it out of politeness? And then, never mind the uneasy drinks and nibbles beforehand, they want to be friends afterwards, when all *I* want to do is go home so that we can discuss it in bed. *That*'s the turn-on for us, really. The sex itself is always dull.' But a woman who does it, and loves it, feels differently. 'I like the fact we got to know each other as people

first. We play regularly with another couple and they've become really good friends as well as sex partners. And because of the sexual thing, we can be completely honest and open with each other.' 'But what do you *do*?' 'Whatever we want – it's not "swapsies", like awful schoolboys – and we never, *ever* nibble on Twiglets.'

It is worth noting, however, that relationships which are strong enough to survive threesomes and moresomes are few and far between.

invitation to an orgy

I went to see the movie *Eyes Wide Shut* with a couple who are enthusiastic orgy-goers. They were, I have to say, *devastated*. 'It's *awful*,' she said. 'Nothing like reality – all those naff masks and silly rituals.' 'And the *women*,' he said. 'They weren't real – all plastic and posing. The point about a *real* orgy is abandonment.' But what about the old saying that the orgy's always next door or last week? 'Not true,' she said, 'Now, with the Internet, anyone can find anything they want, really. But don't bother with Britain – it's terrible. We like France best: Paris. There are sophisticated, civilized clubs there where you'd think it was just a rather classy nightclub until … well, go and see for yourself. You can do just that. If you don't want to actually *do* anything, there's no pressure. Our favourite is called *Chris et Manu*, or there's *Les Chandelles* or – well, just look on the Net. Some people go to Holland but it's a bit jolly for our taste over there. German clubs are interesting – quite dark and wicked. You pays your money …'

'I love watching her being taken by four or five men,' he said, smiling.

'Either she approaches them – just kneels in front of one and unzips him – or I start caressing her, in full view, and pretty soon there are other hands joining in, and then it just goes from there.'

bdsm ...

This stands for bondage, discipline and sado-masochism, and if you think *that's* complicated, you should hear them talking about it. There's a whole other subculture out there – just check out the alt.sex.bondage Usenet group – but what they all have in common is the erotic use of power. BDSM enthusiasts claim power is at the heart of any sexual relationship, and that by *exchanging* that power, so that one person gives it up and the other takes it all, you reach new heights of erotic fulfilment.

'I've been attracted by being helpless ever since I can remember,' one friend told me. 'I used to have these graphic fantasies about being captured and tied to a stake, or tortured by evil executioners. OK, I'm a pervert – I don't mind. But it took me until I was well into my thirties to do anything about it. Then I found my "other half". I have to say we've tried everything you can think of. We've been together for some years now and we don't do those sort of up-front "scenes" any more, but it's still there.'

What's 'everything you can think of?', I wondered. 'You name it,' she said, 'we did it – and do it. From whips, chains, nipple clips, weights and hot wax, to group scenes, bondage and suspension ... as I say, everything. But I must just say this: don't ever, *ever* play with any of that sort of thing unless you're absolutely sure of the person you're with. For me, the essential thing in all this BDSM sex *is not* about power; it's about *trust*, and trusting someone – and putting that trust to the test.'

captain gizmo rides again

Everyone knows about the humble vibrator – or the not-so-humble crystal glass dildo, or the high-tech, three-way Rabbit – but nowadays the world of sex 'toys' (and don't you wish they weren't called that?) can get pretty wild.

What's more, they're not just designed to amuse you when you're having fun by yourself. Any man worth having as a lover is going to be wildly turned on by the sight of his woman pulling out a brand-new gizmo from her shopping and going to work with it straight away. Favourites that friends have come (up) with include:

- **The Love Swing:** 'He can get me in the most unimaginable positions with it. I sit in the swing – it's got these soft, Neoprene straps – and it's just wild. A bed seems soooo boring after that.'
- **A Speculum:** 'I've always had this gynaecologist thing and then my current lover went and bought a speculum and those latex gloves. Well, when he snapped the gloves on I just went crazy. Then he made me lie back with my legs open and took the speculum and ... I just felt so exposed and vulnerable ... 'You'd think it was creepy but in that situation it was hot. Perhaps we should save up for a proper examination couch now.'
- **Enemas:** 'Weird or what? And when he first suggested it ... well, we'd always had a pretty wild sex life, but this – I was appalled. But of course, as always, he talked me round and it was ... it was very powerful. Intimate, invasive, sort of humiliating and yet – I don't know. But ... wow.'
- **The Violet Wand:** 'Bet you don't know what that is. Neither did I. It's a sort of electrical thing ... like a tiny version of those storms-in-a-bottle you get in mail-order catalogues. They used to use it for thinning hair, I think. Anyway, you hold it close to the skin and there are little violet sparks and this incredible tingly buzzing – almost, but not quite, painful. It's like a tiny, ultra-concentrated vibrator. He can drive me insane with it, just sparking it over my clit or my nipples. It's the ultimate teaser ...'

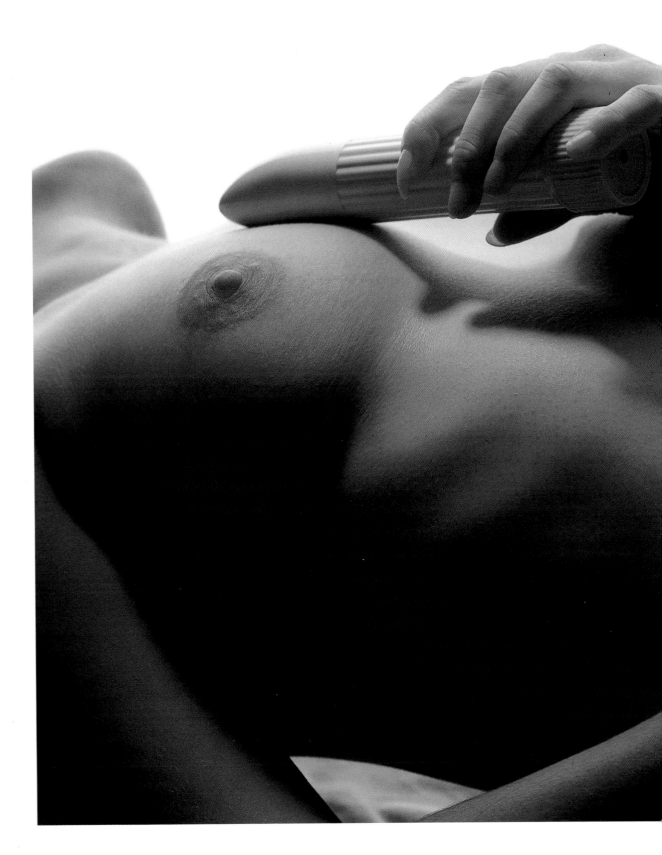

Women who love women

SOME GAY WOMEN have steamy, hot, passionate love lives. They slide themselves into tight leather gear or erotic lace lingerie. Some adore their bodies and the way they look, while others have a bad body image. They have body piercings, use sex toys and do vaginal, oral and anal sex. So what do they want? 'Bountiful, luscious, mind-altering moments of pleasure,' said one lesbian, so there's not much to distinguish them from today's more adventurous *Cosmopolitan* readers, the Ibiza ravers and the hot disco women, who are mostly straight. In fact, most gay women don't do any of the above and, like the majority of the female heterosexual population, lead peaceful, and not especially exciting, love lives.

Lesbian women can be as androgynous or feminine as straight women. They want to love and be loved, and have good sex whenever possible. The difference is that they fancy their own sex.

There are myths about lesbians that still linger. One typical example is that they are women with cropped hair and short, filthy fingernails, who drive Harley-Davidsons and have a job in the local garage. Another is that they are mysterious, artistic and deeply sensitive middle-aged souls, floating about writing novels – Virginia Woolf's *To the Lighthouse*, for example – and then drown themselves.

Of course, gay women have married (Leonard Woolf was a good, supportive husband to Virginia). But these women were not thought of as sexual, although men have always fantasized about erotic lesbian lovemaking. And, what's more, lesbians in Great Britain escaped the hideous legal and social punishments that men faced for loving their own sex, because Queen Victoria, she of the lusty sex life, refused to recognize that lesbians even existed (*as if* women could love women when there were *men* around) – how little she knew.

Today, there are numerous hugely attractive and successful high-profile lesbian role models in sport, business and entertainment. No one bats an eyelid, either, when a lesbian couple have children by artificial insemination – and grandparents are as thrilled and proud as they've always been.

It is estimated that 80 per cent of gay women have slept with men. (Only 20 per cent of gay men have had sex with women.) No wonder 15 per cent of women say that they have and 85 per cent say that they would try it (the Hite Report). Many straight women have experienced lesbian love at certain times in their lives. Women are so tactile, so much more openly affectionate and emotionally close to other women that it doesn't seem like a mighty or shocking leap into the unknown. In fact, many women enjoy gay sex at college and then, in later life, a number of them leave their husbands for a woman, or decide to live openly gay lives.

The most marvellously informative and erotic book on the subject is Felice Newman's, *The Whole Lesbian Sex Book*, subtitled, 'a passionate guide for all of us'. To stir sexual feelings, both straight and gay women should read this one.

5

Modern Sexual Etiquette

The right attitude – for better or worse

THERE ARE 101 wonderful and sad reasons why women have sex – for love, passion, fun or profit, out of curiosity, out of gratitude, for money or revenge, to manipulate or to control. Or for the thrill of it all; because someone asked them and they're flattered; because they feel it's expected of them; or they're forced into it; or they love the power it gives them; or they just love doing it. Often it's because they consciously want to have a child.

If it's sex *you* want with someone – good. If, on the other hand, you *don't* want sex and somebody wants it with you – bad. One of the most exquisitely pleasurable sensations known to woman and man, sex *should* make you *happy*. There are times, of course, when, in return for 'richer and better', or for fear of an impoverished future, or simply unwillingness to be single, wives put up with emotional coldness and have sex with teeth-gritting reluctance. Marital sex, however, like marriage, is regarded as 'a good thing', whatever the quality of the sex or the loving. If modern women (and men) are more reluctant to marry, it may be because they value their independence. They want good, healthy sex lives but they don't want the responsibility of having to be a person for all seasons and they certainly don't want passionless lovemaking.

Comments from a range of married women over 45 included: 'I do it to shut him up,' 'He has no idea about finding pleasure in a woman's body, but I do it to keep him quiet,' 'You have to do it – poor things feel so rejected if you don't,' and even 'We've stopped having sex.' These women probably live with permanent low-grade depression; they dread the bed and the lack of intimacy; and they do not realize they don't have to live like that. Yet it seems that those in dysfunctional marriages would rather discuss *anything* with their partners than how the two of them might improve their sex lives. The kind of tenderness and loving that can infuse long-term relationships never gets a chance in these unhappy partnerships. Quite the opposite, as *consistently* reluctant sex is unhealthy and destructive. No self-respecting, intelligent woman of today should be living that way. So why do so many women do it?

> A long-term relationship with no sex but lots of affection shows far more of the right attitude than unwanted sex that you do simply to 'shut him up'.

While many long marriages are sexless, there are couples in long-term marriages who still enjoy intimate, loving sex. Marriage is an arrangement: you have to make sure that the arrangement suits both of you, not just one of you.

Of course your partner may *sometimes* need or want sex when you're not in the mood. Sometimes sex is a gift, a way to pleasure, comfort or reassure someone you're very fond of. It doesn't always have to be *passionate*. Having a sex life is not all about slit-crotch panties and the cunning use of mirrors. There are times when you have gentle, comforting sex simply because you love the person you're with. It's the affection and the feeling of being valued that's important for both of you; it's about you being in control of your body and your actions, and not feeling blackmailed into sex. 'He'll sulk, and he'll be bad-tempered and won't talk to me. He'll end the marriage if I don't do it,' is *not* the reason to have sex with a difficult, grumpy man who thinks you owe him sexually. But when you love each other, even tired sex at the end of a bad day can be sweet.

Sometimes in a life there'll be Elastoplast, or sticking-plaster, sex – a fling with someone while you're recovering from someone else, or when you are in the middle of a bad love affair – even a bad marriage. You don't fall in love, but there can be a kind of grateful affection and the sex may be surprisingly good. This kind of sex can help restore your confidence before you dust yourself off and move forwards – or go back – with renewed vitality and your sense of humour back in place. Revenge sex can work in the same way. The one you love has behaved badly, or been unfaithful. So, you even up the score. *Yesss*! But it's more potentially explosive, especially if you decide to sleep with one of his friends. Pick a discreet friend. And sex for money? OK, provided *you* know what you're selling and *why*.

Sex is easy during the impassioned months of the Big Romance. You don't get out of bed, your skin glows. You smile foolishly, you're exuberant; you can't stop saying his name all the time. The world around you looks wonderful, if you notice it at all. Mostly, you only notice your lover. That's the time of bonding, magical sex. It could, of course, be the brief but equally golden holiday affair when, in a different place, you become a different woman. Sometimes you remember those holiday weeks all your life – when you strolled along hot beaches, or sat at twinkling harbour cafes. Life's too short not to embrace those perfect moments of romance and sex. But not all sex has to lead somewhere. Sometimes a one-night stand is wonderful. As long as it's what you really wanted to do, and as long as you approached it with enthusiasm and confidence, it reaffirms, encourages and leaves you smiling – that is, as long as you *enjoyed* yourself.

You will learn from your lovers; you learn about men and their vulnerabilities; and you'll start to understand their strengths and weaknesses. You learn to recognize the good ones. Through sex and intimacy, you learn that men want what women want: to love and be loved, to care and be cared for, to have a best friend to confide in and share a joke with, and, for as long as it lasts, to have a good sex life. Loving, enthusiastic sex makes you happy – *very* happy. Why settle for anything less?

If he has the smoothest skin, mention it while you stroke him lovingly. If you love his sense of humour, his big brown eyes, his voice, or he did something that you're proud of, tell him.

28 Unless you are (a) really profoundly in love or (b) achingly in the mood for a quickie, it is worth bearing in mind that a man who habitually does four-minute sex is using you as a lavatory. This is not what women really want – unless they have the self-esteem of a peanut.

29 It is a man with exquisite manners who sends flowers. And it also makes a man feel special to receive flowers from a woman. (But not when one of you is apologizing for bad behaviour.)

30 Hugging does not automatically lead to sex – nor should it have to. Some not-very-bright men presume that it's a sexual signal and, later in the relationship, complain that their partners are not showing them affection. Explain to them that a hug means affection.

31 It's not the end of the world if his penis won't rise to the occasion. It is OK – polite, indeed – to register disappointment, because you would *really* love to have sex with him. You should also try your best oral sex techniques on his wilted penis. If symptoms persist, however, he should swallow his pride and see a doctor.

32 Men are more relaxed when you don't ask them what they're thinking about. Or where they've been, or who with, or why. Don't say, 'What time do you call this?' The fewer questions you ask, the better. Men dislike being interrogated. But isn't the same true of you?

33 Do not overreact when the L-word is introduced into the conversation. Some men say it during sex when they mean, 'Here and now, when my penis is throbbing with excitement, I feel an overwhelming rush of love for you.' Women normally say 'I love you' when they've come to a decision about someone, and they're standing by their decision the next day. It's part of socio-sexual awareness to realize when he means it. *Never* say, 'Do you love me?' You shouldn't have to ask – the answer should be obvious.

34 When you visit his place, it's not a good idea to give him – or his home – a makeover, or to put his things away. A man likes to know where his stuff is, and what looks like a complete mess to you makes perfect sense to him. You're not his mother. Research shows that most men do not want sex with their mother.

35 Unless he invites you to leave things at his place, your toothbrush, moisturizer and make-up remover should not take up residence in his bathroom.

36 Never leave a red satin half-bra stuffed in the front seat of his car. It's a very unsubtle way of staking out your territory.

37 Learn to accept, in moderation, his hobbies and his family, especially his mother. He has to understand that you, too, have your hobbies, family, friends and commitments.

38 Never do with your hands what you can do with your mouth.

39 Occasionally (we've been told) it's polite to fake orgasm. It's like telling a white lie. Apparently, 30 per cent of men have done it. It's equally polite – and more honest – never to fake orgasm.

40 Remember, a small penis is no laughing matter. Sometimes they can expand dramatically and work extremely well. Do not let yourself look surprised; do not wrinkle your face; and do not dive into your bag for a magnifying mirror. Small can be beautiful.

41 Possessive, jealous women are a pain in the butt – as are possessive, jealous men. Relationships need space. You should both take on board that you can't share everything and everyone.

42 A person under pressure, whether at home or at work, cannot always be at their sexual peak. Nor is life all satin sheets and massive, extended orgasms. Go for quality sex when you can.

43 Pamper his penis and remember this well – oral sex will please him more than anything else you'll ever do for him.

44 If one of you really is gay, you need to talk about it – and fast.

45 Do not withhold physical affection if he fails at something – whether it be a promotion, or in his career, or with his business. Sometimes women display their disappointment by refusing to have sex just at the very moment when men are desperate for sexual reassurance.

46 Sex without romance is both depersonalizing and depressing.

47 Tolerance and cheerfulness are the keys to good long-term relationships.

48 Unless what he likes really is a complete no-no, no way, not ever, you should try it, at least twice. It could improve the second time; you might be pleasantly surprised.

49 It seems to be catching on, and you read about it everywhere, but not everyone is doing anal sex and tongues in bums. Don't feel you have to do it unless you're really turned on by the idea.

50 It's always sexual etiquette at the end of the affair to give back the pornographic video in which you played the leading role.

Stockists on the Web

http://ukfetish.info
(*fetish gear and information*)

www.blushingbuyer.com
(*condoms and sex toys*)

www.dark-fashions.net
(*fetishwear, heels and props*)

www.libidex.com
(*a great site for latex*)

www.sensualshopping.com.au
(*lingerie and latex, adult toys and gifts*)

www.sexshop365.co.uk
(*sex toys, clothes, bondage, video and novelties*)

www.sextoyshop.co.uk
(*big selection of dildos, vibrators, etc.*)

www.stockroom.com
(*sex toys and bondage gear*)

www.threethirteen.net
(*click on image, then run cursor over web image until you see the words 'Antimony & lace'. Now click on this*)

www.vibratorsaustralia.com.au
(*sex toys, lingerie, fun and games*)

The Lovers' Guide™

Programme & Product Collection

The series is unique in helping millions around the world to enhance their sex lives and improve their relationships.

The Lovers' Guide™ approach is neither overly medical, nor pornography, but frank, explicit and direct. It is 'sexy, sensual, moral and responsible' [*The Independent*]. Now established as the reliable and acceptable face of sex and relationships, it is the best-seller in its field worldwide. It has been translated into more than 13 languages and has been distributed in 22 countries.

VIDEO PROGRAMMES

LTV001 *The Lovers' Guide: The Art of Better Lovemaking*
63 minutes (1991)
Presented by Dr Andrew Stanway. The original guide to better sex and improving relationships. Contents: Arousal; overcoming shyness, sensual massage; exploring and pleasuring one another; fantasy; making love; sex positions; après sex; sexual problems; STIs; contraception; sex aids; keeping sex alive.

LTV004 *The Lovers' Guide: Making Sex Even Better*
60 minutes (1992)
Presented by Dr Andrew Stanway. Explores more deeply a range of sexual techniques to enrich viewers' love lives. Contents: Sex, desire and communication; erotic times together; prolonging foreplay; advanced foreplay; intensifying intercourse; creative lovemaking positions; sex beyond the bedroom; sex games; first nights; safer sex; banishing boredom.

LTV007 *The Lovers' Guide: Intensifying Lovemaking*
90 minutes (1993)
Presented by Dr Andrew Stanway. The definitive guide to obtaining and intensifying orgasms. Contents: For Her – What is an orgasm?; learning to have an orgasm; improving orgasms; getting your partner's help; better and multiple orgasms. For Him – the sex urge; orgasms and puberty; greater control; increased intensity; getting your partner's help. For Both – orgasmic control; simultaneous orgasms; instant orgasms; orgasms and fantasy; orgasms and sex toys; tantric sex.

LTV4008 *The Lovers' Guide: Massage & Intimacy –*
The Loving Touch
60 minutes (1995)
Presented by Nitya Lacroix. A comprehensive guide to
sensual massage. It demonstrates how to achieve new
levels of intimacy with massage, on the border between
sensuality and sexual arousal, and teaches techniques
for a wonderfully relaxed form of lovemaking. Includes
help in increasing sexual responsiveness and unlocking
the orgasmic reflex.

LTV008 *The Essential Lovers' Guide* [Compilation]
77 minutes (1996)
Consultant Dr Andrew Stanway. A compelling compilation,
which includes sections on keeping relationships alive
and sexy; increasing the length and intensity of male and
female orgasms; being more adventurous; and dealing
with a new relationship.

LTV011 *The Lovers' Guide: Secrets of Sensational Sex*
67 minutes (1999)
Presented by Dr Sarah Brewer. Reveals a wealth of sexual
techniques and sensual skills to take both partners to
new heights of passion and intimacy. Contents: erotic
communication; talking sexily; sex toys for him and her;
exercises for better sex; sensual massage; sex outside
the bedroom; masturbation; oral sex; fetishes; aphrodisiacs.

VC6904 *The Lovers' Guide: What Women Really Want*
51 minutes (2002)
Presented by Dr Sarah Humphery, this is the ultimate
guide to female attitudes to relationships and sex.
Designed for women and their men, the video is
a definitive guide to sexual techniques that enhance a
woman's pleasure for women. It covers what women
really want in life, from their bodies, from sex, from
their lover and from their relationship.

PUBLICATIONS

The Lovers' Guide
(Lifetime/Eddison Sadd Editions. Pub: Pan Macmillan)
128pp (1992)
Consultant: Dr Andrew Stanway.
Based on the best-selling *Lovers' Guide* video, this
book has sold over 200,000 copies. It shows young
couples how to take the first steps towards sexual
intimacy with loving care and confidence, and teaches
more experienced partners how to revive and improve
their lovemaking techniques.

The Lovers' Guide Encyclopaedia
(Pub: Bloomsbury) 256pp (1996)
Edited by Doreen Massey.
A definitive guide to all aspects of sexuality and
relationships. Sections include: sexual facts; feelings
and behaviour; sexual outlook; sex and culture; and
a dictionary of sexual terms.

*The Lovers' Guide: Understanding and Exploring the
Art of Lovemaking*
(Pub: Marshall Cavendish) 85 x 28pp (1993–4)
A full-colour weekly guide to the art of lovemaking,
building into a whole compendium of the subject. This
partwork explores all aspects of sex and relationships,
including: creative lovemaking; shedding inhibitions;
psychology; sex in society; cults; sexual problems; etc.

MULTIMEDIA

The Interactive Lovers' Guide CD-Rom
(Waddingtons) (1993)
An early foray into making sex interactive. Lots
of information, coupled with games and quizzes,
which seeks to explore a new approach to
understanding sexuality.

The Lovers' Guide Interactive CD-Rom
(YITM – Yorkshire TV/Thompson) (1996)
An interactive and explicit guide to sex and relationships
with over 40 minutes of live-action video and over 400
colour images. It allows users to access a guide to a
more varied and exciting sex life; to discover their own
sexual profile and create a personalized programme for
happiness; to consult an advice line on intimate concerns
and problems; and provides a comprehensive database
of sex and sexual practices.

The Lovers' Guide Website

www.loversguide.com
An on-line guide with real-life stories, information on
sexual health, FAQs and a question-and-answer forum.

Various soundtrack recordings have been released by
Pickwick. An audio book of *The Lovers' Guide* is currently
in development.

A range of games has been devised for interactive
television. The first, with Static (Playjam Channel – Sky)
in 2001, was the most commercially successful game
they had ever launched.

Index

Picture Credits

The publishers would like to thank the following sources for their
kind permission to reproduce the pictures in this book:

Page 23 Courtesy Ann Summers,
Page 31 Carlton Books Limited,
Page 33 TR Carlton Books Limited, BL Courtesy Durex Limited,
Page 43 BR Carlton Books Limited,
Page 47 Carlton Books Limited,
Page 63 Carlton Books Limited,
Page 66 Carlton Books Limited,
Page 67 TR Carlton Books Limited,
Page 73 Carlton Books Limited,
Page 77 Carlton Books Limited,
Page 79 Carlton Books Limited,
Page 80 Carlton Books Limited,
Page 84 Mother & Baby Picture Library,
Page 94 Carlton Books Limited,
Page 95 Carlton Books Limited,
Page 99 Carlton Books Limited,
Page 108 Courtesy Ann Summers,
Page 109 Carlton Books Limited,
Page 120 Carlton Books Limited.

Every effort has been made to acknowledge correctly and contact the
source and/or copyright holder of each picture, and Carlton Books Limited
apologizes for any unintentional errors or omissions which will be corrected
in future editions of this book.